# The Content of American History as Taught in the Seventh and Eighth Grades; an Analysis of Typical School Textbooks

# UNIVERSITY OF ILLINOIS BULLETIN

Issued Weekly

Vol. XIII          AUGUST 21, 1916          No. 51

Entered as second-class matter December 11, 1912, at the post office at Urbana, Illinois,
under Act of August 24, 1912.

# UNIVERSITY OF ILLINOIS
# SCHOOL OF EDUCATION

## BULLETIN No. 16

## The Content of American History

### As Taught in the

## Seventh and Eighth Grades

BY

W. C. BAGLEY and H. O. RUGG

PUBLISHED BY THE
UNIVERSITY OF ILLINOIS
URBANA

# The Content of American History

## As Taught in the

# Seventh and Eighth Grades

## An Analysis of Typical School Textbooks

BY

W. C. BAGLEY and H. O. RUGG

WITH THE COÖPERATION OF

MRS. H. O. RUGG AND MRS. W. C. BAGLEY; MISSES HELEN CLARK, MARGARET COBB,
ELIZABETH FULLER, MALI LEE, AND OLIVE PAINE; MESSRS.
A. J. BEATTY AND J. H. JOHNSTON

# TABLE OF CONTENTS

# THE CONTENT OF AMERICAN HISTORY AS TAUGHT IN THE SEVENTH AND EIGHTH GRADES

## AN ANALYSIS OF TYPICAL SCHOOL TEXTBOOKS

## I

## INTRODUCTION

In 1912, one of the writers of the present paper was requested by the Committee on Economy of Time of the Department of Superintendence (National Education Association) to make an investigation of "minimal essentials" in elementary geography and history  He presented the problem to a graduate seminary in educational values in the University of Illinois.  During the second semester of 1912-13, the problem was discussed and several possible methods of determining minimal essentials in the various school subjects were devised and tested  None of these methods seemed, however, to be adequate to the solution of the problem in so far as geography and history were concerned  During the following year, the problem was submitted to another group of graduate students.  Two methods of approach were subjected to a preliminary test  One of these was based upon the assumption that the relative value of historical and geographical facts may be at least roughly determined by the frequencies with which references and allusions to these facts appear in periodical literature. The other method involved a "rating" by competent authorities of the relative significance of geographical and historical data.  Typical results obtained by an application of each of these methods formed a part of the report of the Committee at the Cincinnati meeting of the Department of Superintendence in 1915, and were published as Chapter IX of the *Fourteenth Yearbook*[1] of the National Society for the Study of Education.

During the course of these preliminary efforts, it became increasingly apparent that a succinct statement of the *present content* of elementary history and geography was needed as a basis for further work. This need was intensified by the discussions of the seminary relative to the meaning of the term "minimal essentials" Under the assumption that the minimal content of geography and history as taught in the elementary school should include the geographical and historical data with which *everyone* should be familiar, —the facts and principles which might be assumed as part of the culture *common to all of the people,*—the need for knowing what elements of historical and geographical knowledge are now, and have been in the immediate past, actually part of the common pabulum of elementary instruction assumed prime importance. An analysis and comparison of the textbooks extensively used in the seventh and eighth grades seemed likely to meet this need more adequately than any other procedure

This analysis was undertaken for elementary history by the members of the seminary Twenty-three texts in history published during the past fifty years and representing four rather distinct successive periods of publication were obtained. It was hoped that "first editions" could be used in every case, but this was impracticable Indeed, some of the books that were at the outset included were omitted from the final list, either because it was doubtful whether they were intended primarily for the grades in question, or because the publication of successive editions, the difficulty of determining the changes made in these editions, and the inability to obtain first editions made it impossible to state in what periods of publication they rightfully belonged. The writers believe, however, that the textbooks that are represented in the present report are typical of seventh and eighth grade work during the periods that are covered The list includes some of the books that have had a very wide circulation, although one or two books very extensively used were necessarily omittted, because the publication period of the available edition could not be determined. Included in the list, also, are at least three books used extensively in the southern states and representing the southern point of view, and at least one book apparently written with the needs of the Catholic parochial schools especially in mind

*The Significance of Elementary Textbooks in National History.* The work of the seventh and eighth grades commonly represents the

[1]University of Chicago Press, 1915.

first serious and systematic instruction in history. The earlier study of this subject is largely based either upon oral instruction by the teacher (instruction which is very variable in both quantity and quality) or upon very elementary texts which are usually written in the story form, which emphasize primarily biographical materials, and which often lack sequential organization. With the degree of maturity attained by seventh and eighth grade pupils, however, the systematic study can be profitably undertaken, and the textbook in history with materials fairly well standardized and fairly uniform throughout the country becomes the dominant agency of instruction

And the influence of this elementary work is fundamental and far-reaching It cannot be doubted that points of view, attitudes, and prejudices engendered at this time will tend to persist even if the detailed facts are largely forgotten It is these enduring outcomes of the initial study of history that will form the perspective through which the next generation will view the problems of national life. If the elementary course is fundamentally at fault, this perspective will inevitably be distorted and its distortion will be reflected in fallacious collective thinking and ineffective collective conduct. Other factors in addition to the initial study of history will determine the thought and the conduct of the coming generation, but no other subject taught in the schools today can have the influence exerted by this initial systematic study of national history in the seventh and eighth grades in so far as the attitude of the people toward national issues is concerned. Even those pupils who go on to the secondary and higher schools, and who there pursue more advanced courses in American history, will continue to be influenced by this initial study,—as any teacher of history in high school or college can testify. For the great majority whose systematic study of history is limited to this initial course, the seventh and eighth grade instruction is fundamentally determining.

Under the conditions that are general in American elementary and secondary schools, it is the textbook that forms the basis of the instruction in history. "In the majority of American schools it determines the facts to be taught and the manner of teaching them."[1] What goes into the elementary textbook in history is therefore a matter of vital significance. The relative emphasis that is given to different events, the names that are kept alive from generation to generation, the points of view that the textbooks reflect, the ideals with which they will tend to indoctrinate their immature readers,—all of these

---

[1] H Johnson *Teaching of History in Elementary and Secondary Schools* New York, 1915 P 269

factors demand consideration in an adequate study of textbooks in history.

*Aim of the Present Study.* It is the purpose of the present paper to present facts and raise problems rather than to set forth conclusions, or outline solutions. The following pages reveal fairly accurately the present content of this basic historical instruction and the significant changes that this content has undergone in the past half century. Both the principal events and the characters associated with them have been listed with reference to the relative emphasis which the different texts lay upon them in so far as this emphasis can be determined by proportions of space and frequencies of reference.

*This paper does not attempt to pass judgment upon the authenticity or the historical reliability of the textbook materials.*[1]

*Method.* At the outset, the following method was adopted the number of words in each of the books was carefully computed by one person; each book was then assigned to an individual for analysis, with the expectation that the topics and the amount of space devoted to each could be determined for each book and the results brought together later for comparison. A brief trial proved this method to be unsatisfactory, and the procedure was so modified that each member of the group was assigned a single period or epoch and asked to analyze each of the books with reference to this period, noting the topics and names common to all of the books, the topics and names common to at least three fourths of the books, and the topics and names common to at least one half of the books. The brief statement of preliminary results published in the *Fourteenth Yearbook* is based upon this analysis.

At the conclusion of this work, the results seemed to justify a careful "checking" in order to reduce the error that is unavoidable when so many individuals collaborate in work of this sort. This checking was done with great care by Dr and Mrs. H. O. Rugg during the summer of 1915, and included a reworking of all of the periods except that of the Civil War; the topical analysis for this period is based almost entirely upon the report of the original collaborator

Certain discrepancies between the data given in the *Fourteenth Yearbook* and the data presented in the following pages are to be explained by the fact that the reworking of the material gave in some instances slightly different results Few of these discrepancies, however, are so wide as to be significant.

---

[1] The writers are indebted to Professors E B Greene and C M Thompson for suggestions and criticisms from the historian's point of view regarding the material presented in this paper

## II

## THE TEXTBOOKS REPRESENTED IN THE STUDY

For purposes of comparison, the twenty-three books[1] forming the basis of the analytic study may be grouped according to date of copyright into four classes, as follows.

CLASS I.  *Books representing the years from 1865 to 1874 (inclusive)*

A. B Berard  *School History of the United States* (Revised edition). Philadelphia  H. Cowperthwaite, 1866  (Copyright dated 1865)  Pp viii, 303, 81,200 words

Marcius Willson  *History of the United States from the Earliest Discoveries to the Close of the Great Rebellion in 1865*  .  New York. Ivison, Blakeman, Taylor & Co  No date on title-page  (First copyright dated 1853, copyright of edition used dated 1866)  Pp 459, 121,400 words.

Charles A Goodrich.  *History of the United States of America for the Use of Schools*  Revised and brought down to the present time by William H Seavey. Boston  Brewer and Tilleston  No date on title-page  (Copyright dated 1867).  Pp 320, 28 (28 pages of appendices and index) ; 36,400 words

John J Anderson, Ph D  *A Grammar School History of the United States*  .  New York· Clark & Maynard, 1880.  (Copyright dated 1874, no changes from copyrighted edition have been indicated except that two articles have been added on territorial growth and civil progress).  Pp. 212, 91 (91 pages of appendices, questions for topical study, and index) ; 39,800 words.

CLASS II.  *Books representing the years from 1881 to 1888 (inclusive).*

M. E Thalheimer  *The New Eclectic History of the United States*  New York  American Book Company.  No date on title-page  (Copyrights dated 1881, 1890, 1899, 1902, 1904)  It is stated in the preface that "corrections" have been made in the successive editions, that the style has been simplified, and that "a few matters beyond the comprehension of children have been omitted" ; in the light of these statements, the book has been placed in this period)  Pp. 400, xlv (45 pages of appendices and index) ; 69,800 words.

Joel Dorman Steele, Ph D , F G S , and Esther Baker Steele, Litt.D :  *A Brief History of the United States* (Barnes's "Brief History")  New York: American Book Company  No date on title-page  (Copyrights dated 1871, 1879, 1880, 1885)  Pp 410, 57,700 words

Edward Eggleston:  *A History of the United States and Its People*  For the use of schools. New York  American Book Company.  No date on title-page.  (Copyright dated 1888)  Pp. xii, 416; 58,200 words.

---

[1]The selection of the textbooks was entirely "random"  In addition to recent books furnished by the publishers to the library of the School of Education, as many older texts as were offered by certain secondhand dealers were purchased and all of these that had apparently been written for the grades in question were used in the study

CLASS III [1]  *Books representing the years from 1890 to 1904 (inclusive).*

Edward S Ellis, A M  *School History of the United States*  Revised edition  Chicago  The Werner Company  No date on title-page  (Copyrights dated 1892, 1894)  Pp 369, 50,900 words

Josiah H. Shinn  *History of the American People*  New York  American Book Company  No date on title-page  (Copyrights dated 1893, 1899)  Pp 454, 82,900 words

William M Davidson  *A History of the United States*  Chicago. Scott, Foresman & Company, 1904  (Copyright dated 1902)  Pp xxiv 548, 88,716 words

Thomas Bonaventure Lawler, A M, LL D  *Essentials of American History*  Boston  Ginn & Company  No date on title-page  (Copyright dated 1902); 69,400 words

D H Montgomery  *The Leading Facts of American History*  Boston: Ginn & Company, 1893  (Copyright dated 1890)  Pp. xii, 360, lxvii; 106,400 words.

William H Mace  *A School History of the United States*  Chicago: Rand, McNally & Company  No date on title-page  (Copyright dated 1904).  Pp xcv, 465, x, 108,900 words

Thomas Wentworth Higginson:  *Young Folks' History of the United States*  New York  Longmans, Green, and Co, 1904  (Copyrights dated 1875, 1886, 1902; there is some doubt as to whether this book should be included in this or in the preceding period, from the "internal evidence", however, it would seem either that the earlier editions had been extensively revised or that the later developments had been anticipated; structurally it belongs to the period indicated by the latest copyright)  Pp vi, 400, 33 (33 pages of questions), 78,800 words.

William Estabrook Chancellor  *A Text-Book of American History*  New York  Silver, Burdett & Company  No date on title-page  (Copyright dated 1903, note dated 1904, at the end of the preface, indicates that certain typographical corrections were made at that time)  Pp 653, 106,100 words

CLASS IV.  *Books representing the years from 1906 to 1912 (inclusive):*

William A Mowry and Blanche S Mowry  *Essentials of United States History*  New York  Silver, Burdett & Company  No date on title-page  (Copyrights dated 1906, 1911)  Pp x, 382, 52 (52 pages of appendices and index), 87,100 words

James Albert Woodburn, Ph D., and Thomas Francis Moran, Ph D ·  *American History and Government.*  A Text-Book on the History and Civil Government of the United States  New York  Longmans, Green, and Co, 1907  (Copyright dated 1906, reprints listed 1906, 1907); 127,100 words

[1]It should be said that some of these books (and probably some of those placed in Class II) have been extensively revised, and that, if later editions had been used, they would have been listed with the books of Class IV.

John Bach McMaster    *A Brief History of the United States*  New York·
American Book Company   No date on title-page. (Copyright dated 1907).
Pp 434, xxx (30 pages of appendix and index) , 76,756 words

Edward Channing   *A Short History of the United States*  For school
use  Revised in consultation with Susan J Ginn   New York  The Macmillan
Company, 1912   (Copyrights dated 1900, 1909, reprints listed 1900, 1901 (2),
1902 (2), 1904, 1906, 1907, 1908, "new and revised edition," 1909, reprints listed
1911, 1912). Pp xx, 407, xxiv (24 pages of appendices and index) , 73,000 words

Charles Morris   *School History of the United States*  Philadelphia. J.
B Lippincott Company  No date on title-page  (Copyrights dated 1909, 1911)
Pp xix, 451, xxxiii (33 pages of appendices and index) , 102,800 words

Edmond S Meany  *United States History for Schools*  New York: The
Macmillan Company, 1912  (Copyright dated 1912). Pp xviii, 587, 117,700
words

Two additional books were used in making some of the determinations.

W F Gordy  *A History of the United States for Schools*   New York·
Charles Scribner's Sons, 1911  (Copyrights dated 1898, 1899, 1910, 1911)  Pp
xxviii, 484  (From the preface  "In this new edition the history has been
brought down to date  Although many changes in the text have not been found
necessary, yet, whenever in the interests of a more useful book such changes
have seemed advisable, they have been unhesitatingly made")

Marguerite Stockman Dickson·  *American History for Grammar Schools.*
New York: The Macmillan Company, 1915.  (Copyright dated 1911, reprints
listed 1912, 1913, 1914 (2), 1915 (3) ). Pp xviii, 539, lii

Certain facts regarding the authorship of school histories deserve mention  At least six of the books were written by professors of
history in colleges and universities,—some of whom are historians of
high standing.  These six books belong either to Class III or to Class
IV,—that is, they are books that have been published since 1890
Eight of the books were written by what may be termed "professional"
textbook writers whose right to rank as historical scholars would probably be open to serious question.  Four of the books were prepared
by public-school administrators.  Three of the books were prepared
by men of letters, at least two of whom (Higginson and Eggleston)
have a place in American literature.

The tendency toward elementary-textbook authorship by writers
who have already won recognition for specialized scholarship in the
field of American history is worthy of note, although it should be said
that the text which has probably been most extensively used in the
schools of the northern states during the past decade was written by a
superintendent of city schools.

## III

## GENERAL CHARACTERISTICS OF THE BOOKS

a) *Organization.* The typical organization of these textbooks is upon the basis of large topics, each representing a chronological unit or epoch. The number of these topics varies from four in Mowry to fourteen in Davidson and sixteen in Shinn. Of the seventeen books that are topically organized, nine present the materials under six, seven, or eight large headings (each of these three numbers being represented by three books). There seems to be no distinct tendency toward either more or fewer large topics in the recent books as compared with the older books; indeed the number of topics seems to be determined largely by individual whim or preference  The number of large divisions that would provide the best organization from the standpoint of economy in learning could be determined experimentally, but this type of investigation has yet to be undertaken. The following are samples of the methods of subdivision:

*Berard* (1867)
I    Discoveries
II.   Settlements
III   Intercolonial wars
IV   Revolution
V.   National development
VI   Great rebellion

*Mowry* (1911)
I    The colonies
II   The revolution
III.  The nation
IV.  The new nation

*Barnes (Steele)* (1885)
I   Introduction (prehistoric)
II.  Early discoveries and settlements
III  Development of the colonies
IV.  The revolution
V.   Development of the states
VI   Civil war
VII.  Reconstruction and passing events

*Channing* (1909)
I.    Discovery and exploration
II.   Colonization
III.  A century of colonial history
IV   Colonial union
V    The war of independence
VI   The critical period
VII.  The Federalist supremacy
VIII. The Jeffersonian republicans
IX   War and peace
X.    The national democracy
XI.   Slavery in the territories
XII   Secession (1860-1861)
XIII  The war for the union
XIV.  Reconstruction and reunion
XV.   National development

b) *Appendices* All of the recent and most of the earlier books reprint both the Declaration of Independence and the Federal Constitution as appendices. Davidson inserts each at its chronologically appropriate place within the text  Lists of the presidents and tables showing the dates of admission and other facts regarding the several states are also included as appendices in the majority of the books Documents other than the Declaration and the Constitution are found (as appendices) as follows  Articles of Confederation (Meany), Washington's Farewell address (Anderson), the Mayflower compact (Mace); Lincoln's Gettysburg speech (Mowry)  A few of the books include as appendices chronological tables, topical outlines, and lists of questions.

c) *References and Bibliographies* The books of Class I (1865-1875) contain no references for outside reading  Berard gives an occasional footnote reference to Bancroft, but does not cite title of book, Goodrich includes as footnotes many quotations from authorities, usually naming both the author and the title of the book from which the quotation is made, but sometimes contenting himself with the author's name; Berard follows the older custom of prefacing each chapter with a quotation, usually a stanza of poetry or a verse from the Bible. The books of Class II (1881-1888), however, furnish numerous bibliographical references, and practically all of the more recent books furnish adequate bibliographies either at the close of the sections or at the close of the book  Many of the recent texts provide both references to authorities with pages indicated, and lists for the home reading of pupils. In no other feature is the improvement in the construction of the textbooks during the past fifty years more noticeable than in connection with the references and suggestions for wider reading.

d) *Questions, Outlines, and Problems* Seventeen of the twenty-three books provide study questions  In the earlier books, these are commonly distributed in foot-notes throughout the book or on the margins of the pages (Willson)  In the later books they are either given at the close of the chapter or sub-section, or collected as an appendix; there is no prevailing mode, although the most favorable location for study questions could readily be determined by experiment. Topical outlines or summaries are found in seventeen of the books, usually at the close of chapters or sections, but occasionally (as chronological tables or extended topical outlines) at the close of the book.

The emphasis that has been placed upon the use of the problem during the past few years is reflected in the later texts. The following are typical questions taken from books published prior to 1904:

"What British officer had entered Virginia?—Who was sent to defend it?—What city did Washington design to attack?—What did he do instead?—How did Washington prevent pursuit?—When did the French and American forces unite at Yorktown?"—Berard (1867), p. 165.

"Where did Cornwallis go after the failure of his southern campaign?—What kind of a war did he wage in Virginia?—Why did he retire to Yorktown?—What plan did Washington now adopt?—Describe the siege of Yorktown."—Barnes (Steele) (1885), p. 322.

"What did Cornwallis do when he reached Virginia?—What general was in command of the Americans in Virginia?—How did Lafayette show ability?—What did Washington do?—Who commanded the French army that accompanied Washington?—What part did the French fleet play in the siege of Yorktown?"—Eggleston (1888), p. 190.

"What French army had landed?—What led to the defeat of Cornwallis?—When did he surrender?—Describe his surrender."—Higginson (1902), p. 20 (appendix).

"Was the end near at hand?—What did Cornwallis do?—What of Washington and Rochambeau?—The French fleet?—What was the strength of the allies?—When was the attack opened?—What was the feeling between the French and the Americans?—When did Cornwallis surrender?—Describe the scene."—Ellis (1894), p. 301.

Marked improvement in the construction of the study question, particularly the introduction of the "problematic" element, is first noticed in Mace's text published in 1904. The contrast between the foregoing questions and the following is sufficiently striking to suggest that a forward step of no small magnitude was then taken in the teaching of history.

"When Lafayette wrote to Washington that the British were in Yorktown, what did Washington discover?—Give reasons why one army in our day could not march from West Point and surprise another in Yorktown.—Picture the scenes in Philadelphia and the surrender scene.—Imagine yourself Cornwallis and tell your thoughts and feelings at the surrender.—Treat Lafayette and Washington in the same way.—Make a list of the effects of the surrender." (Mace, p. xxxi—appendix).

This type of problem question is now the rule in the elementary texts in history; for example:

"How did Lafayette outwit Cornwallis?—Why is Yorktown called the climax of the Revolution?"—Meany (1912), p. 229.

"What were the advantages and disadvantages of Cornwallis's position at Yorktown?—Was Cornwallis wise in occupying this position?—Give reasons for your opinion—Compare the surrenders at Saratoga and Yorktown—Compare Burgoyne and Cornwallis.—Write an account of the three men who, in your view, did most to make good the Declaration of Independence."—Turpin (1911), p 416

"*Resolved* That a republic is the best form of government [Suggested question for debate]. In the form of a journal written by a girl during the Revolution, tell how she aided the patriot cause."—Turpin (1911), p 417

In Mrs. Dickson's text the present tendency is clearly shown in the variety of pedagogical helps that are appended to each chapter. The following list, referring to the events that closed the Revolution, is typical of this plan of treatment.

### "THINGS TO REMEMBER

"1. The news of Cornwallis's surrender was received with dismay by the British ministry

"2 England's European wars were also unsuccessful

"3 The people of England were anxious to have peace

"4 A treaty of peace was finally concluded in 1783, England acknowledging the independence of the United States.

### "THINGS TO READ

[Five references are enumerated here ]

### "THINGS TO DO

"1 Find the meaning of *revolt, havoc, knaves*

"2 Review the struggle for independence, using the outline on page 242 as a basis

"3 Review Washington's career as commander-in-chief What qualities did he show?

### "FOR YOUR NOTEBOOK

"Make a map to show the boundaries of United States territory according to the treaty.

"Copy the treaty for your notebook

"Write about some hero of the Revolution (Do not forget that the common people, who were neither generals nor statesmen, the soldiers whose highest service was obedience to orders, the women who struggled to till the little farms and to support their families while 'father was gone to war,' even the boys and girls who did the small things which fell to their lot to do in helping the great cause, were as much heroes in their way as the brilliant and the famous )"

e) *Style.* It is difficult to characterize the style of elementary textbooks in history. Every textbook writer, especially if he is writing for children, aims to combine brevity, clarity, and vividness The

texts in history that have had a wide circulation have been marked
by an easy, fluent, straightforward style. This is generally true of the
earlier books as well as of those more recently published. At the
same time, there have been noteworthy changes in the type of treatment. What may be called "straight narrative" is somewhat less in
evidence in the recent books, although it still quite naturally constitutes the dominant mode of composition. The narrative, however, is
· more frequently amplified by description; and expository paragraphs
referring particularly to economic and social problems have become
more numerous. In a few of the older books, the tendency to "fine
writing" is noticeable, but sentences like the following have not
strongly characterized books published since 1875:

"At peace with foreign nations, and blessed with almost unexampled pros-
perity in the various departments of agriculture, commerce, and manufactures,
our course is steadily onward in the march of national greatness." (Willson,
1866, p. 371).
"Washington, who felt deeply the wrongs of the army, yet whose noble
spirit was grieved that they should tarnish their fair fame by deeds of violence,
used all his influence to calm their excited feelings, and succeeded, in great
measure, in quieting their fears." (Berard, p. 170).

Steele's text ("Barnes's Brief History") was probably the book
most widely used in the northern states during the years 1885-1890.
It owed some of its popularity no doubt to its vivid and picturesque
style, the most striking feature of which is the short sentence. The
following passage referring to the surrender of Cornwallis is typical:

"Both parties felt that this surrender virtually ended the war. Joy per-
vaded every American heart. All the hardships of the past were forgotten in
the thought that America was free. The news reached Philadelphia at the
dead of night. The people were awakened by the watchman's cry, 'Past two
o'clock and Cornwallis is taken.' Lights flashed through the houses, and soon
the streets were thronged with crowds eager to learn the glad news. Many
wept, and the old door-keeper of Congress died with joy. Congress met at
an early hour, and that afternoon marched in solemn procession to the Lu-
theran church to return thanks to Almighty God." (Steele, p. 140).

During the two most recent publication-periods, a more distinct
effort toward clarity of thought-connections is to be noted. Expository
and descriptive sentences and paragraphs are more frequently brought
in to supplement the narrative. "Causal relationships," while not
entirely neglected in the earlier texts, are now given larger emphasis.
The following citations illustrate this tendency:

"It will be remembered that during the time of the Embargo and the
War of 1812 the country, being cut off from foreign trade, was obliged to build

its own mills and factories to produce whatever manufactured goods were needed for home use As the streams flowing down the New England hillsides furnished excellent water-power, the business men of that region gradually invested their capital in manufacturing instead of commerce. Until 1816 duties had been levied on goods from foreign countries mainly for revenue to pay the expenses of the national government These duties furnished only incidental protection to American manufacturers Such a system is called 'a tariff for revenue with incidental protection'

 After the war closed, however, and trade was resumed with foreign countries, our markets became flooded with foreign goods, especially from England Labor was so much cheaper in England than in this country that her merchants could sell goods to the United States at a lower price than American manufacturers could afford to sell them

"Our manufacturers naturally called for a higher tariff on the goods that could be made to advantage in American mills and factories These imported goods would then cost so much in the United States that the American manufacturer could afford to undersell the foreigner and still make a profit Such a tariff is said to encourage home industries, or to protect American manufacturers from foreign competition. It is therefore called a protective tariff." (Gordy, p 252).

"It was impossible, however, for agriculture, manufacturing, or commerce to make any very great advance without better facilities for transportation The heavy, clumsy, and uncomfortable stage-coach was the principal vehicle for land travel It was a huge, boxlike affair, without glass windows, doors, or steps, and provided with side curtains of leather to be used in stormy weather. These rude coaches, drawn by bony horses in harness of rope, lumbered along at the rate of forty miles a day in summer and twenty-five in winter. The day, however, began at three o'clock in the morning and ended at ten at night. In 1783 two of these coaches handled the passenger traffic and a part of the freight as well, between New York and Boston In many instances in stage-coach travel the passengers were obliged to get out and push in order to get the vehicle out of the mud. Spots of quicksand were marked by stakes to warn travelers to avoid them, and in many instances it was necessary to go through fields and take an entirely new course The great rivers were not bridged, and the coaches crossed on the ice in winter and on rude ferryboats in summer In the breaking-up time of the spring and during the early winter, when the ice was not strong, the passage was often very dangerous" (Woodburn and Moran, p. 255).

In general, it would seem that the earlier texts aimed at picturesqueness and vividness in a measure that does not characterize the more recent books. Some of the latter, indeed, seem to be rather studiously matter-of-fact.

f) *Anecdotal Materials.* The place that anecdotes should have in the content of elementary history is a puzzling question, but there can be no doubt of the very significant rôle that the anecdote has hitherto played, and there can be little doubt of the efficiency of the anecdote in insuring the persistence and recall of historical information—and misinformation.  The problem is both historical and pedagogical:  (1) What anecdotes are both true and typical of general conditions? and (2) How may the anecdote be made an effective center about which to associate facts that would otherwise not be remembered, and how shall the teacher avoid giving irrelevant details of the anecdote an importance that they do not deserve?

It is clear from our analysis of the textbooks that the use of anecdotes has been declining.  To take a single period rather rich in anecdotal materials (the period of the colonial wars), we find that the average number of anecdotes referring to this period in the books published since 1906 is just one half the number in the books published between 1865 and 1874.  This period of the colonial wars also furnishes very good illustrations of what may be called "standard anecdotes."  Three fourths of the twenty-three books, for example, relate the dying words of Wolfe and Montcalm, while nearly one half of them refer, with but slight variations in the language used, to the tradition that Washington had two horses shot from under him and that four musket balls passed through his clothing.  Six of the twenty-three books relate that Wolfe recited Gray's "Elegy" just prior to the capture of Quebec.

The period 1783-1812 is also rich in anecdotal materials.  At least nine of the books tell in practically the same words that, when Washington was on his way to the first inauguration, young girls strewed flowers in his path.  That Mrs. Adams lost her road while on her first journey to the new city of Washington is deemed important enough for mention by several writers.  Of a somewhat different order are the aphoristic statements which seem to have been especially numerous and particularly "pat" during these formative years.  The majority of the books repeat Pinckney's famous expression: "Millions for defense, but not one cent for tribute."  Other favorite quotations are Webster's highly figurative tribute to Hamilton[1]; a similar tribute to Marshall[2]; Franklin's reference to the rising sun; and the statement said to have been made by Napoleon at the time of the Louisiana purchase.[3]

The tendency to draw explicit moral lessons from historical events and anecdotal materials shows a significant decline in the books pub-

[1]"He smote the rock of our national resources, and abundant streams of revenue poured forth; he touched the dead corpse of public credit, and it sprang upon its feet."

[2]"He found the Constitution paper, and made it power; he found it a skeleton and clothed it with flesh and blood."

[3]"This accession of territory strengthens forever the power of the United States, and I have just given to England a maritime rival which will sooner or later humble her pride."

lished since 1890 The collaborator who examined the books with reference to this point finds that the following virtues and vices have been referred to most frequently by the textbook writers who have made explicit statements of praise or censure; (the analysis was limited to the period of colonial development including the colonial wars) ·

Heroism
Sympathy (with reference to the Acadian exile)
Cruelty (instances among both the Indians and the colonists)
Faith in divine assistance
Confidence
Obstinacy and vanity (Braddock is the "stock" illustration)
Rashness and cowardice (Abercrombie)

The variations in judgment may be illustrated by the treatment of the Acadian exile Eleven writers distinctly condemn the English; four state both sides with an obvious attempt at impartiality; one explicitly leaves open the question of justice or injustice; and one definitely attempts to justify the English policy.

g) *Pictures* All of the twenty-three books are illustrated. The very earliest books contain relatively few pictures, but the texts that were published between 1875 and 1890 are quite as fully illustrated as those that have appeared within the past decade There has, however, been a marked change in the character of the illustrations. The imaginative and highly idealized wood-cuts, which lent a specious charm to the earlier texts, and which reached their climax between 1880 and 1890, either have quite disappeared from the recent texts, or are at most limited to reproductions that have value because of their artistic merit or because of an honest effort at a reconstruction based upon authentic source materials Most of the pictures used today, however, are photographic reproductions of the actual source materials themselves,—costumes, implements, contemporary documents (including maps and drawings), and the like. Some of the improvement is due, of course, to recent developments in the art of photo-engraving. but much of it may be traced to the more adequate ideals of sincerity and honesty in historical instruction.

A comparison of typical pictures may be helpful. In one of the texts belonging to the second publication-period, the following illustrations appear within the space of few pages ·

A highly imaginative wood-cut, purporting to represent Champlain among the Indians.

A highly colored lithograph depicting the landing of a marvelously attired European gentleman, and his reception by a group of fine looking, swarthy savages

A group of "gentlemen" settlers.
A wood-cut entitled the "Landing of the Ninety Honest Girls."
A picture supposed to represent the marriage of Pocahontas.

Within a similar number of pages also dealing with the period of colonization, Turpin's text (1911) contains the following pictures:

A drawing of the tobacco plant.
A picture of the ruins of Jamestown.
Reproduced photograph of the statue, "The Puritan."
The *Mayflower* under sail. (Wood-cut).
Reproduced photograph of Boughton's "Pilgrims going to Church."
Portrait of John Winthrop.
Drawings of snow-shoes and moccasins.
Line drawing of a New England blockhouse.
Picture of a New England farmhouse built in 1676.

h) *Maps.* The maps have increased in number and greatly improved in quality during the period under consideration. More efficient methods of printing have again been in part responsible for the increase and the improvement, but more adequate conceptions of the importance of map study in history have also played an important part. In the earlier books the small outline-map was chiefly employed, and principally in connection with military campaigns. In the books published since 1890, larger lithographed maps are general, but the smaller outline-map is still retained. The map now becomes an important means of portraying territorial growth and expansion, although this use was anticipated in some of the earlier books.

## IV

## THE SIZE AND SCOPE OF THE TEXTBOOKS AND THE DISTRIBUTION OF SPACE AMONG THE LARGER TOPICS

The twenty-three books vary in length from 36,000 words (Goodrich) to 139,900 words (Davidson), the average being 84,320; eight books, however, contain more than 100,000 words. In general, the shorter books belong to the earlier periods, although there are some significant exceptions. (Willson's text, for example, contains 121,400 words). The averages in the different periods as represented by the following table are somewhat misleading, as the range in each period is wide:

## TABLE I

| | Average number of words | Range |
|---|---|---|
| Four books representing the years 1865 1874 . | 69,700 | 36,400–121,400 |
| Three books representing the years 1881-1888 . . | 61,900 | 57,700– 69,800 |
| Nine books representing the years 1890-1902 | 88,716 | 50,900–139,900 |
| Seven books representing the years 1904-1912 . | 97,737 | 73,000–127,100 |

In order to determine the relative emphasis given in the various periods of publication to the larger divisions of American history, the number of words in each of the books relating to each of the several periods was proportioned to the total number of words in the book. The results for each book and the averages by periods are as follows:

## TABLE II

| | Discovery and exploration | Colonial development | Colonial wars | Pre-revolution | Revolution | 1783-1812 | 1812-1861 | Civil war | 1865 to date of publication | Check |
|---|---|---|---|---|---|---|---|---|---|---|
| *Class I* | | | | | | | | | | |
| Goodrich | 6.0 | 12.2 | 4.7 | 5.2 | 18.4 | 6.8 | 18.4 | 23.8 | 2.51 | 98.0 |
| Anderson | 7.5 | 15.8 | 6.8 | 2.4 | 15.0 | 9.27 | 20.9 | 12.75 | 15.4 | 105.8 |
| Berard | 2.3 | 29.4 | 4.5 | 1.5 | 20.0 | 4.28 | 13.9 | 14.8 | | 100.3 |
| Willson | 7.0 | 28.0 | 6.5 | 3.3 | 17.0 | 5.05 | 14.5 | 14.5 | | 96.1 |
| **Average** | **5.7** | **21.3** | **5.6** | **3.1** | **17.6** | **6.4** | **16.9** | **18.8** | **8.95** | **101.4** |
| *Class II* | | | | | | | | | | |
| Barnes | 10.8 | 18.5 | 4.6 | 1.8 | 17.0 | 3.67 | 18.7 | 17.6 | 11.44 | 103.5 |
| Eggleston | 5.0 | 26.8 | 6.3 | 1.8 | 14.0 | 12.07 | 13.3 | 14.3 | 7.29 | 100.8 |
| Thalheimer | 8.0 | 14.8 | 3.6 | 2.0 | 21.0 | 9.4 | 14.8 | 10.75 | 15.3 | 99.7 |
| **Average** | **7.93** | **20.0** | **4.83** | **1.86** | **17.3** | **8.2** | **15.6** | **14.2** | **11.3** | **101.3** |
| *Class III* | | | | | | | | | | |
| Ellis | 7.8 | 15.7 | 3.6 | 1.6 | 12.0 | 6.54 | 25.8 | 19.0 | 9.15 | 101.8 |
| Shinn | 16.0 | 18.9 | 4.4 | 2.32 | 18.0 | 8.0 | 15.8 | 11.7 | 8.5 | 103.6 |
| Davidson | 11.0 | 15.9 | 3.5 | 3.1 | 10.0 | 7.23 | 23.4 | 12.5 | 11.29 | 97.9 |
| Lawler | 14.0 | 15.7 | 3.4 | 2.8 | 13.0 | 3.75 | 23.6 | 9.7 | 13.54 | 99.5 |
| Montgomery | 13.0 | 23.8 | 2.6 | 2.2 | 9.3 | 5.89 | 16.9 | 10.1 | 16.3 | 99.9 |
| Thompson | 11.6 | 14.2 | 2.0 | 3.8 | 11.5 | 7.6 | 19.8 | 14.1 | 14.1 | 99.5 |
| Mace | 6.0 | 20.2 | 3.4 | 4.53 | 9.0 | 9.4 | 23.1 | 10.55 | 13.76 | 99.9 |
| Higginson | 13.0 | 27.1 | 5.3 | 5.7 | 11.6 | 7.64 | 12.8 | 8.8 | 7.86 | 99.8 |
| Chancellor | 8.0 | 15.7 | 2.6 | 4.1 | 12.5 | 5.03 | 10.9 | 10.5 | 38.8 | 98.1 |
| **Average** | **11.15** | **17.96** | **3.42** | **3.35** | **11.87** | **6.78** | **19.12** | **11.88** | **14.87** | **99.9** |
| *Class IV* | | | | | | | | | | |
| Mowry | 6.0 | 13.7 | 2.4 | 4.4 | 15.0 | 10.74 | 19.7 | 11.5 | 16.4 | 99.8 |
| Woodburn and Moran | 7.0 | 11.0 | 3.6 | 4.6 | 7.4 | 27.8 | 23.6 | 10.0 | 9.63 | 104.5 |
| McMaster | 4.1 | 21.3 | 5.2 | 2.4 | 10.0 | 15.17 | 23.2 | 7.0 | 13.13 | 101.5 |
| Channing | 6.3 | 10.5 | 2.3 | 6.0 | 7.8 | 18.25 | 24.9 | 11.7 | 10.20 | 98.0 |
| Morris | 14.0 | 19.8 | 4.3 | 4.4 | 8.4 | 7.77 | 16.0 | 10.0 | 16.73 | 101.4 |
| Turpin | 9.9 | 15.3 | 3.1 | 3.3 | 9.1 | 10.4 | 20.7 | 11.9 | 18.45 | 102.15 |
| Meany | 10.6 | 20.1 | 4.8 | 3.7 | 9.5 | 9.1 | 19.3 | 9.5 | 16.7 | 102.9 |
| **Average** | **8.27** | **15.95** | **3.67** | **4.11** | **9.58** | **14.17** | **21.01** | **10.22** | **14.45** | **101.43** |

While the proportions of space indicated in the table are only approximations, it is clear from the final "checking" column that the approximations are reasonably close  Subject to the caution necessitated by variations, certain tendencies revealed by the table may be accepted as at least suggestive —

a)   The gradual but consistent decline in the proportion of space devoted to each of the three war-periods would not be significant were it paralleled by a similar decrease in the proportion of space devoted to other of the earlier periods, for the more recent books have a longer total period to cover  As a matter of fact, however, the proportion of space devoted to exploration and discovery, to the pre-revolutionary period, to the years 1783-1812, and to the period from 1812 to 1861, not only has not declined but on the contrary has generally increased in the more recent books.  Thus the contraction has been largely confined to the three war-periods and to the period of colonial development, and more significantly to the former.

b)   Of the early periods receiving increased emphasis in the most recent books (the books of Class IV) that between 1783 and 1812 reveals the most significant increase.  It will be noted that five of the seven books of Class IV devote a larger proportion of space to this period than does any of earlier books except that of Eggleston.

c)   The increase in the proportion of space devoted to the years 1812-1860 would be even more marked if the War of 1812 and the Mexican war had been treated separately  Combining the average proportions for both of these wars, the following results are obtained: Class I, 9 52% ; Class II, 5 09%, Class III, 4 94% ; Class IV, 4 41%  Subtracting these from the corresponding per cents for the total period 1812-1861, the average proportions of space devoted to the *non-military* affairs of this period are found to be as follows:

| | |
|---|---:|
| CLASS I . .. .. .. . .... .. .. ... .. .. .. ... ... | 7 4% |
| CLASS II . .. . . .. .. . . .. .. ... ... | 9 6% |
| CLASS III .. .. .. . ... .. .. ... .. . .. .. .. .... ... | 14 2% |
| CLASS IV . .. . .. . .. .. . .. . ... .. .. | 16 6% |

(d)   The books of Class I taken as a group devote to the five war periods (the Colonial wars, the Revolution, the War of 1812, the Mexican war, and the Civil war) more than one half of the total text-book space.  In the aggregate these five war periods cover forty-eight years, or about one fifth of the time elapsing between the founding of Jamestown and the close of the Civil war.  The most recent texts devote but little more than one fourth of their space to these five war-periods. The decline began with the publication-period, 1881-1888, as the following averages show:

Books of Class I (1865-74) give to the five war-periods on the average 51.5% of their space.

Books of Class II (1881-88) give to the five war-periods on the average 41.4% of their space.

Books of Class III (1890-1902) give to the five war-periods on the average 32.0% of their space.

Books of Class IV (1904-12) give to the five war-periods on the average 28.4% of their space.

Nor are the differences among the four classes of books in respect of the treatment of the latest period (1865-1912) sufficient to account for the lessening emphasis upon military events, as the following table shows:

| Books of | Average per cent of total space devoted to the period from 1865 to date of publication |
|---|---|
| Class I | 8.95 |
| Class II | 11.3 |
| Class III | 14.87 |
| Class IV | 14.45 |

As showing the actual space devoted to wars (as contrasted with proportion of entire space), the following figures are significant:

| Books of | Average number of words in book | Average number of words devoted to wars |
|---|---|---|
| Class I | 69,700 | 35,895 |
| Class II | 61,900 | 25,626 |
| Class III | 88,716 | 28,389 |
| Class IV | 97,737 | 27,757 |

# V

## THE PERIOD OF DISCOVERY AND EXPLORATION

The typical treatment of this period comprises the following topics:

a) America before Columbus
b) European background
c) Spanish explorations
d) English explorations
e) French explorations
f) Dutch explorations
g) Portuguese explorations

a) The treatment of America before Columbus has been a feature of most of the books from the earliest of the four periods under consideration, but relatively less emphasis is given to this topic in the books of Class IV (1904-1912) than in the books of the preceding period. The Norsemen are referred to in more than three fourths of the books; and some reference to the Mound builders and the Indians finds a place in more than one half of the books.

b) Reference to the European background is not a feature of the books published prior to 1880, but the emphasis has increased steadily since that time, the books of Class IV devoting on the average 11.8% of the space of the whole period to this topic as compared with 4.7% in the books of Class III and 2.3% in the books of Class II. The principal sub-topics have reference to (1) the crusades, (2) the condition of geographical knowledge in Europe in the fifteenth century, and (3) the blocking of the older trade-routes with the fall of Constantinople.

c) The Spanish explorers have the largest average proportion of space in the books of all periods except in those of Class I which give this honor to the English explorers. The general distribution of emphasis is shown in the following table; the figures represent the average per cent of the total space of the period devoted to each group:

TABLE III

|           | Spanish | English | Dutch | French | Portuguese |
|-----------|---------|---------|-------|--------|------------|
| CLASS I   | 9.5     | 19.6    | 3.0   | 11.0   | 0.6        |
| CLASS II  | 37.0    | 14.9    | 2.0   | 12.0   | 0.7        |
| CLASS III | 31.0    | 9.7     | 2.0   | 11.0   | 1.6        |
| CLASS IV  | 29.0    | 12.7    | 3.0   | 9.8    | 1.6        |

The number of persons whose names are mentioned in connection with this period varies from nineteen (in Berard) to sixty-nine (in Davidson); the median is thirty-seven. Of these names, only five appear in all of the books: Columbus, John and Sebastian Cabot, Balboa, and Sir Walter Raleigh  Ten additional names appear in three fourths or more of the books  These are: Vespucci, Drake, Ponce de Leon, Gilbert, Magellan, Cortez, de Soto, Cartier, White, and Verrazano. Eight names are added if at least one half of the books are considered: Menendez, de Narvaez, Forbisher, Gosnold, Champlain, Ribeau, Coronado, and de Gama  Thus, although thirty-seven different persons are named in the median book, only twenty-three names find a place in from one half to three fourths of these elementary texts  Measured by the average proportion of space devoted to the exploits and achievements of these persons in books of Class IV, and giving to Columbus an arbitrary rank of 100, the most significant names and the relative "weight" attached to each are as follows

| | | | |
|---|---|---|---|
| COLUMBUS | 100 | VESPUCCI | 15 |
| RALEIGH | 26 | VERRAZANO | 13 |
| CHAMPLAIN | 20 | BALBOA | 10 |
| JOHN CABOT | 17 | DE LEON | 10 |
| SEBASTIAN CABOT | 17 | CORONADO | 10 |
| MAGELLAN | 16 | DRAKE | 8 |
| DE SOTO | 16 | CORTEZ | 8 |

This order would not be significantly modified if the books of Class III were included.

## VI

## THE PERIOD OF COLONIAL SETTLEMENT AND DEVELOPMENT

The general distribution of emphasis in the treatment of this period is represented in the following table  The figures represent the average per cent of the *total book* given in each class of textbooks to each of the large topics

TABLE IV

| | Government and politics | Indian relations | Religion | Education | Other features of social life |
|---|---|---|---|---|---|
| CLASS I | 7 19 | 1 63 | 0 89 | 0 12 | 1 34 |
| CLASS II | 6.1 | 1.34 | 0 86 | 0 15 | 1.35 |
| CLASS III | 7.83 | 1 38 | 0 95 | 0.28 | 1 86 |
| CLASS IV | 7.83 | 0 53 | 0 49 | 0 35 | 1 25 |

The significant tendencies here are the decreased emphasis upon Indian relations and religious difficulties and the somewhat increased emphasis upon education in the most recent texts. It will be noted that the emphasis upon government and politics remains practically constant.

As to the general treatment of the period, it is sufficient to say that, in the large majority of the texts, the various colonies are considered separately,—some books following a chronological order of development, others beginning with New England and proceeding through the Middle to the Southern colonies. There are certain groups of facts that seem to have been so fairly well standardized as to form the basis of common topics in three fourths of the books. These topics are listed below, together with additional topics that are found in at least fifty per cent of all the books. The figures represent the average per cent of the entire book devoted to the topic in each of the four classes of texts, (these topics are not always given in chronological sequence) ·

## TABLE V

### A  PLYMOUTH AND MASSACHUSETTS BAY COLONIES

| Topics common to at least 75% of the books | Average per cent of space devoted to each topic in each publication period | | | | Additional topics common to 50% of the books | Average per cent of space devoted to each topic in each publication period | | | |
|---|---|---|---|---|---|---|---|---|---|
| | I | II | III | IV | | I | II | III | IV |
| Mayflower compact | 0 24 | 0 15 | 0 15 | 0 19 | Development of Plymouth . . .. | 0 46 | 0 15 | 0 19 | 0 17 |
| Mass Bay settlement | 0 32 | 0 17 | 0 23 | 0 36 | Indian relations . | 0 13 | 0 26 | 0 17 | 0 33 |
| Charter difficulties. | 0 24 | 0 20 | 0 36 | 0 24 | Anne Hutchinson and | | | | |
| Witchcraft ... . . . | 0 51 | 0 25 | 0 17 | 0 11 | Roger Williams | 0 23 | 0 23 | 0 26 | 0 11 |
| European background Pilgrims and Puritans . .. ... . | 0 35 | 0 51 | 0 39 | 0 38 | Founding of Harvard university | 0 12 | 0 20 | 0 19 | 0.13 |
| People of the colonies. | .0 10 | 0 18 | 0 14 | 0 18 | | | | | |

### B  NEW HAMPSHIRE AND MAINE

| | | | | | | I | II | III | IV |
|---|---|---|---|---|---|---|---|---|---|
| | | | | | Settlements | 0 19 | 0 25 | 0 21 | 0.07 |
| | | | | | Mason and Gorges | 0 12 | 0 09 | 0 07 | 0 11 |
| | | | | | Division . . . | 0 25 | 0 00 | 0 07 | 0 05 |
| | | | | | Union with Mass | 0 20 | 0 09 | 0 13 | 0 11 |

### C  RHODE ISLAND

| | I | II | III | IV | | I | II | III | IV |
|---|---|---|---|---|---|---|---|---|---|
| Roger Williams . . . | 0 39 | 1 17 | 0 16 | 1 06 | Providence ... .. | 0 06 | 0 04 | 0 09 | 0 12 |
| | | | | | Newport . . . | 0 11 | 0 06 | 0 10 | 0 05 |

### D  CONNECTICUT

| | I | II | III | IV | | I | II | III | IV |
|---|---|---|---|---|---|---|---|---|---|
| Hooker's emigration from Massachusetts | 0 15 | 0 11 | 0 13 | 0 12 | Dutch settlements . | 0 16 | 0 23 | 0 18 | 0 13 |
| | | | | | 1st written constitution | 0 25 | 0 15 | 0.12 | 0 12 |
| Settlements at Hartford, Windsor, etc. | 0.31 | 0.13 | 0 13 | 0 17 | Union of colonies . . | 0 20 | 0.14 | 0 20 | 0 22 |
| | | | | | Andros . | 0 21 | 0 24 | 0 17 | 0 16 |
| Pequod war ... .. | 0 39 | 0 30 | 0 21 | 0 19 | Charter Oak | 0 14 | 0 25 | 0 12 | 0 11 |
| | | | | | King Philip's war | 0 52 | 0 33 | 0 35 | 0 22 |

### E  NEW YORK

| | I | II | III | IV | | I | II | III | IV |
|---|---|---|---|---|---|---|---|---|---|
| First settlement | 0 22 | 0 17 | 0 23 | 0 32 | Development of New Amsterdam | 0 07 | 0 10 | 0 10 | 0 15 |
| Peter Stuyvesant | 0 32 | 0 08 | 0 18 | 0.18 | Dutch rule | 0 45 | 0 27 | 0 23 | 0 16 |
| English conquest and rule . . . | 0 38 | 0 31 | 0 31 | 0 28 | Geisler's revolution | 0 21 | 0 13 | 0 16 | 0 18 |
| | | | | | Patroons . .. .. | 0 07 | 0 11 | 0 23 | 0 14 |

**F. NEW JERSEY**

Grants to Berkeley and Carteret ......0.09 0.08 0.12 0.08
Division into East and West New Jersey......0.18 0.09 0.08 0.11
Quakers and Puritans..0.16 0.12 0.08 0.07

Settlements ......0.15 0.11 0.14 0.11
Creation of royal colony ......0.15 0.00 0.13 0.14

**G. PENNSYLVANIA**

William Penn ......0.22 0.18 0.13 0.17
Founding of Philadelphia ......0.14 0.08 0.16 0.10
"Great Treaty" ......0.22 0.24 0.20 0.08

Charter ......0.10 0.00 0.13 0.14
The "Holy Experiment" ......0.14 0.14 0.17 0.18
"Mason and Dixon" line ......0.07 0.00 0.10 0.11
Growth of the colony....0.00 0.19 0.34 0.12

**H. DELAWARE**

Settlements ......0.31 0.08 0.15 0.17

Transfer to Pennsylvania ......0.08 0.11 0.11 0.13

**I. MARYLAND**

The Calverts ......0.12 0.30 0.11 0.12
Claiborne's rebellion......0.14 0.23 0.20 0.23
Toleration act ......0.08 0.17 0.18 0.12

Charter and government ......0.56 0.14 0.34 0.27
Settlement at St. Mary's ......0.03 0.03 0.07 0.08

**J. VIRGINIA**

Settlement of Jamestown ......0.28 0.64 0.17 0.19
First assembly ......0.14 0.16 0.23 0.20
Government ......0.77 0.50 0.45 0.43
"Starving time" ......0.25 0.20 0.15 0.14
John Smith ......0.48 0.32 0.23 0.17
Slavery introduced......0.23 0.10 0.13 0.16
Bacon's rebellion ......0.34 0.19 0.26 0.36

Charters ......0.18 0.17 0.23 0.17
Navigation acts ......0.24 0.20 0.14 0.14
Indian troubles ......0.30 0.30 0.28 0.25
Pocahontas ......0.30 0.24 0.16 0.14
Character of settlers....0.35 0.08 0.43 0.15
Wives for the settlers..0.09 0.16 0.17 0.13
Tobacco culture ......0.02 0.15 0.18 0.12

**K. THE CAROLINAS**

Settlements ......0.25 0.24 0.16 0.15
Locke's "Grand Model" ......0.10 0.17 0.23 0.06

Grants ......0.10 0.26 0.12 0.09
Settlement of Charleston ......0.07 0.08 0.11 0.08
Division into North and South ......0.27 0.19 0.18 0.23
Huguenots ......0.14 0.10 0.14 0.17
Rice culture and indigo..0.10 0.13 0.19 0.12

**L. GEORGIA**

Oglethorpe's plan ......0.12 0.22 0.24 0.17
Spanish invasion ......0.25 0.14 0.13 0.08

Settlement of Savannah ......0.09 0.06 0.12 0.08

The period of colonial growth is the least satisfactory "epoch" of American history to treat pedagogically. The simultaneous development of thirteen separate colonies, each with its own problems, and with relatively few interests in common prior to the Revolution, is very difficult for a pupil of grammar-school age to envisage. At the same time, historians have apparently felt that it is necessary to give to each of the colonies at least a passing reference,—and in some books most of the references are little more than this. The proportion of space devoted to this period has generally declined during the past fifty years (from an avereage of 21.5% of the entire book in texts of Class I to an average of 15.95% in texts of Class IV), but there are wide variations among the several books of each period.

In respect of the proportions of space given to the topics listed in Table V, a few significant movements may be noted. In the recent books, King Philip's war receives less than one half of the attention that the earlier books accorded to it, the Pequod war has also fallen off in the same proportion; the space devoted to witchcraft has steadily declined, and the picturesque incidents and traditions associated with the names of John Smith and Pocahontas have lost more than half of their older prominence. In the case of no topic, character, or event does a significant increase in emphasis appear,—even where we might perhaps expect such an increase, as, for example, in the topics concerning religion and other features of the social life.

The median number of names mentioned in the discussion of this period is 53; the range is from 32 (in Channing) to 116 (in Willson) Nine names are common to all of the books; (no significance attaches to the order in which the names appear).

| | |
|---|---|
| John Smith | Peter Stuyvesant |
| Sir William Berkeley | George Carteret |
| John Winthrop | William Penn |
| Roger Williams | James Oglethorpe |
| Sir Edmund Andros | |

Fourteen additional names are found in at least three fourths of the books; again the order is not significant:

| | |
|---|---|
| John Mason | Sir Thomas Dale |
| Sir Ferdinando Gorges | John Rolfe |
| George Calvert | Nathaniel Bacon |
| William Claiborne | Massosoit |
| Pocahontas | King Philip |
| Powhatan | John Endicott |
| Lord de la Ware | Lord Berkeley |

Nineteen additional names are found in one half or more of the books, (the order is not significant).

| | |
|---|---|
| Lord Say-and-Seal | Thomas Hooker |
| Lord Brooke | John Carver |
| John Davenport | William Bradford |
| Peter Minuit | William Brewster |
| William Kieft | Miles Standish |
| Jacob Leisler | Canonicus |
| John Locke | Annf Hutchinson |
| Cecil Calvert | John Harvard |
| George Yeardley | "Mason and Dixon" |

It is again noticeable that the number of names common to one half of the books or more (43) is smaller than the number mentioned in the median book (53)

# VII

## THE COLONIAL WARS

The space devoted to the colonial wars is distributed as follows; the figures represent the average per cent of the total space of the book for the books of each publication period:

TABLE VI

|  | I | II | III | IV |
|---|---|---|---|---|
| King William's war | 0.50 | 0.53 | 0.45 | 0.35 |
| Queen Anne's war | 0.67 | 0.40 | 0.30 | 0.40 |
| King George's war | 0.48 | 0.24 | 0.29 | 0.19 |
| French and Indian war | 3.79 | 2.70 | 2.97 | 2.75 |

In the treatment of the first three wars there are no topics that are common to all of the books. The topics common to at least three fourths of the books and additional topics common to one half or more of the books are given in the following table; the average per cent of the entire book given to each topic is indicated for each of the publication periods but only for the more important topics:

TABLE VII

A. KING WILLIAM'S WAR

| Topics common to at least 75% of the books | Publication-periods | | | | Topics common to 50%-74% of the books | Publication-periods | | | |
|---|---|---|---|---|---|---|---|---|---|
|  | I | II | III | IV |  | I | II | III | IV |
| Cause of the war | 0.25 | 0.13 | 0.37 | 0.37 | Canadian expedition | 0.09 | 0.12 | 0.07 | 0.44 |
| Phipps at Port Royal | 0.13 | 0.12 | 0.10 | 0.09 | Treaty of Ryswick | 0.13 | 0.23 | 0.09 | 0.48 |
|  |  |  |  |  | Schenectady burned |  |  |  |  |
|  |  |  |  |  | Attack on Haverhill |  |  |  |  |
|  |  |  |  |  | European background |  |  |  |  |

B. QUEEN ANNE'S WAR

| | I | II | III | IV | | | | | |
|---|---|---|---|---|---|---|---|---|---|
| Causes | 0.52 | 0.09 | 0.15 | 0.16 | Walker's expedition | | | | |
| Attack upon Port Royal | 0.16 | 0.05 | 0.07 | 0.04 | Attack upon Deerfield | | | | |
| Treaty of Utrecht | 0.21 | 0.08 | 0.15 | 0.09 | | | | | |

C. KING GEORGE'S WAR

| | I | II | III | IV |
|---|---|---|---|---|
| Causes | 0.26 | 0.13 | 0.04 | 0.13 |
| Siege of Louisburg | 0.67 | 0.77 | 0.39 | 0.35 |
| Treaty of Aix-la-Chapelle | 0.16 | 0.19 | 0.16 | 0.33 |

The treatment of the French and Indian war comprises six topics that are common to all of the books:

TABLE VIII

| Topics common to all texts | Average per cent of entire book devoted to each topic in each publication-period | | | |
|---|---|---|---|---|
| | I | II | III | IV |
| Causes | 0.39 | 0.25 | 0.44 | 0.49 |
| Washington sent as messenger to the French | 0.50 | 0.34 | 0.30 | 0.21 |
| Building of Fort Duquesne | 0.11 | 0.07 | 0.08 | 0.07 |
| Braddock's defeat | 0.44 | 0.39 | 0.31 | 0.47 |
| Conquest of Quebec | 0.86 | 0.48 | 0.50 | 0.49 |
| Treaty of Paris and territorial readjustments | 0.13 | 0.24 | 0.18 | 0.23 |

The additional topics common to at least three fourths of the texts and to at least one half of the texts are shown in Table IX.

TABLE IX

| Additional topics common to at least 75% of the books | I | II | III | IV | Additional topics common to 50%-74% of the books |
|---|---|---|---|---|---|
| Forbes's expedition against Ft. Duquesne | 0.22 | 0.11 | 0.04 | 0.10 | Surrender of Montreal |
| Exile of Acadians | 0.30 | 0.17 | 0.16 | 0.11 | Pontiac's war |
| Ft. Necessity | 0.09 | 0.10 | 0.05 | 0.07 | Naming of Pittsburgh |
| Pitt and the political situation in England | 0.11 | 0.09 | 0.07 | 0.10 | Attack at Great Meadows |
| Reduction of Louisburg | 0.11 | 0.07 | 0.03 | 0.04 | Albany convention |
| Abercrombie's expedition against Ticonderoga | | | | | Surrender of Ft. William Henry |
| Abandonment of Ticonderoga and Crown Point | | | | | Expedition against Crown Point |

It will be noted that from the time of the early discoveries there is no significant number of topics common to *all* of the texts until we reach the French and Indian war. The outstanding importance of the six common topics relating to this war is clear at a glance, and it would be difficult to find in Table IX a single topic that would rank in significance with those of Table VIII. At the same time there is a fair equivalence in importance between the topics common to at least three fourths of the texts in the treatment of all four wars.

There are few significant changes of emphasis in the successive publication-periods. The decreasing attention given to the Acadian exile is noteworthy, as is the increased emphasis accorded to the causes of the French and Indian war. Washington's first expedition to

Fort Duquesne is given in the later books less than one half of the proportion of space that it had in the books of Class I. As the first appearance of Washington upon the stage of American history, however, this event will probably hold its place among the "constants."

One hundred seventy-three different persons are mentioned in the various texts as associated with this period. The range is narrower than in the preceding periods,—from 9 (in Thompson) to 43 (in Willson). The median book mentions 20 names, but *only three* are common to all of the books; these are:

> WASHINGTON
> BRADDOCK
> WOLFE

Three additional names are common to at least three fourths of the books:

> MONTCALM
> WILLIAM PITT
> DINWIDDIE

Six more names (in addition to Longfellow, who is mentioned in connection with the Acadian exile) are found in at least one half of the books:

SIR WILLIAM JOHNSON          PONTIAC
GENERAL AMHERST              BENJAMIN FRANKLIN
GENERAL ABERCROMBIE

# VIII

## THE PREREVOLUTIONARY PERIOD

The treatment of this period between the Treaty of Paris and the Battle of Lexington is, in respect of topics, much more uniform throughout the several texts than any of the preceding periods. Ten topics common to all of the books are listed:

TABLE X

| Topics common to all books | Average per cent of whole book for each publication-period | | | |
|---|---|---|---|---|
| | I | II | III | IV |
| Policy of England toward the colonies.... | 0.38 | 0.34 | 0.49 | 0.66 |
| Stamp act | 1.02 | 0.49 | 0.83 | 0.84 |
| Boston massacre | 0.14 | 0.14 | 0.20 | 0.15 |
| Boston "Tea party" | 0.27 | 0.21 | 0.22 | 0.22 |
| Boston port bill | 0.22 | 0.15 | 0.25 | 0.22 |
| First Continental congress | 0.24 | 0.13 | 0.25 | 0.21 |
| "Writs of assistance" | 0.20 | 0.14 | 0.11 | 0.16 |
| New taxes | 0.29 | 0.18 | 0.23 | 0.28 |
| Results of England's policy of taxation.... | 0.34 | 0.17 | 0.40 | 0.49 |

The topics common to smaller proportions of the books were not worked out for this period

The only significant change of emphasis in the successive publication-periods is the increased attention given to the policy of England toward the colonies.

Despite the brevity of the period, one hundred eighteen different names are mentioned in the twenty-three texts. The range is from eleven (in Ellis) to fifty-three (in Davidson). The median book mentions twenty-three names—or three more than are mentioned by the median book in connection with the preceding period.

Of the 118 different names, only one is found in all of the books Giving this name the arbitrary value of 100, the proportionate distribution of emphasis in so far as this can be determined by frequency of mention is as follows·

a) *Mentioned in all books*
    Patrick Henry ... .. ... .    ... .. .. .. .. .. .. .. .. . 100
b) *Mentioned in at least three fourths of the books*
    Samuel Adams . .. .. .     .. ... . .. .. .. .. . . 87
    William Pitt .         .    . .    .. .. .. .. . ... 47
    General Gage .  .. .. ... ... .. .. .. ........... .. .. .... ..... . 44
    James Otis        . .. ... .  . .. . .. .. .   . . 41
c) *Mentioned in at least one half of the books*
    George III ..      .. ... .   . . .  .. .. .. . 52
    Benjamin Franklin .. .. .. ... .. .. .. ...... .. ... ... . 33
    Washington . .. .. ..    . .. .. ... .. .  . .. .. 21

## IX

## THE WAR OF THE REVOLUTION

It will be recalled from Table II that the proportion of space devoted to the Revolution has steadily declined during the four publication-periods until, in the recent books, it is but little more than one half of the proportion in the books of Class I  Some of the important shifts in emphasis with reference to large topics are revealed in the following table; the figures here, unlike those of the tables immediately preceding, represent both the average per cents of the space devoted *to the period* and the average per cents of the *total* space:

TABLE XI

*Publication-periods*

| | I | II | III | IV | |
|---|---|---|---|---|---|
| Political, social, and geographical conditions in the colonies.............. | 0.56 | 1.07 | 0.75 | 0.95 | (Percent of book) |
| | 3.2 | 6.2 | 6.4 | 9.9 | (Per cent of period) |
| European background ............................ | 0.14 | 0.38 | 0.53 | 0.2 | (Percent of book) |
| | 0.8 | 2.2 | 4.5 | 2.0 | (Percent of period) |
| Military and naval operations............. | 14.96 | 10.0 | 8.2 | 6.6 | (Percent of book) |
| | 85.0 | 58.0 | 69.0 | 69.0 | (Percent of period) |
| Illustrative and vivifying details........ | 0.7 | 0.29 | 0.33 | 0.5 | (Percent of book) |
| | 4.0 | 1.7 | 2.8 | 5.3 | (Percent of period) |

The important increase in emphasis is in connection with the political and social conditions in the colonies; the significant decrease is in connection with military and naval operations.

As one would expect, the number of topics common to all of the books is much larger than in the preceding periods. Table XI lists these common topics.

TABLE XII

| Topics common to all books | Average percent of total book given to each topic in the four publication-periods | | | |
|---|---|---|---|---|
| | I | II | III | IV |
| Lexington and Concord ............................ | 0.35 | 0.54 | 0.49 | 0.41 |
| Bunker Hill ................................................. | 0.48 | 0.54 | 0.44 | 0.28 |
| Siege of Boston........................................... | 0.31 | 0.24 | 0.15 | 0.11 |
| Washington Commander-in-Chief ............ | 0.21 | 0.10 | 0.11 | 0.10 |
| Declaration of Independence..................... | 0.28 | 0.62 | 0.47 | 0.33 |
| Ticonderoga ................................................ | 0.12 | 0.14 | 0.11 | 0.04 |
| Long Island ................................................ | 0.35 | 0.50 | 0.20 | 0.15 |
| Retreat through New Jersey...................... | 0.22 | 0.29 | 0.15 | 0.13 |
| Battle of Trenton ...................................... | 0.27 | 0.19 | 0.21 | 0.10 |
| Battle of Princeton ................................... | 0.28 | 0.15 | 0.14 | 0.13 |
| Valley Forge .............................................. | 0.14 | 0.43 | 0.20 | 0.11 |
| Burgoyne's campaign ................................ | 0.15 | 0.11 | 0.51 | 0.54 |
| Monmouth ................................................... | 0.40 | 0.21 | 0.17 | 0.10 |
| Arnold's treason ........................................ | 0.71 | 0.71 | 0.38 | 0.22 |
| Camden ........................................................ | 0.12 | 0.17 | 0.18 | 0.09 |
| Cowpens ...................................................... | 0.12 | 0.14 | 0.12 | 0.08 |
| Guilford Court House ............................... | 0.10 | 0.14 | 0.12 | 0.08 |
| Yorktown ..................................................... | 0.70 | 0.38 | 0.31 | 0.22 |
| Treaty of Paris .......................................... | 0.12 | 0.14 | 0.17 | 0.17 |

The following additional topics are common to at least three fourths of the books:

## TABLE XIII

| Topics common to at least 75% of the books | Average per cent of total book devoted to each topic in the four publication-periods | | | |
|---|---|---|---|---|
| | I | II | III | IV |
| Invasion of Canada ... ... ... ... ... . | 0 44 | 0 29 | 0 18 | 0 11 |
| Fort Moultrie .. ... ... .. ... ... ... . | 0 22 | 0 21 | 0 13 | 0 07 |
| Brandywine and Germantown . . . | 0 12 | 0 17 | 0 16 | 0 12 |
| Stony Point . ... ... ... ... .. | 0 19 | 0 68 | 0 10 | 0 08 |
| Marion, Pickens, Sumter .. ... ... ...... .. | 0 63 | 0 43 | 0 29 | 0.11 |
| Eutaw Springs . .. . . .. ... | 0 15 | 0 86 | 0 07 | 0 05 |
| King's Mountain ... ... . .. ... ..... . . .. | 0 10 | 0 05 | 0 09 | 0 10 |
| Capture of Savannah ... ... ... ... .... ..... . | 0 05 | 0 04 | 0 05 | 0 04 |
| Paul Jones and naval exploits .. ... . | 0 31 | 0 25 | 0 24 | 0 24 |
| Fall of Charleston .. . ... . ... . | 0 17 | 0 08 | 0 10 | 0 07 |
| Expedition of George Rogers Clark... ... . | 0 02 | 0 02 | 0.20 | 0 13 |

It will be noted that the emphasis given to campaigns and battles has declined steadily and most consistently. The only marked instance of an increased emphasis is in connection with Burgoyne's campaign, the proportion of space here having more than trebled in spite of the steady decrease in the proportion of space given to the period as a whole  The increased attention to Clark's expedition and the larger emphasis of the Treaty of Paris are also significant.

Three hundred one different persons receive mention in the twenty-two texts that were examined with reference to this matter [1] The range is from 28 (in Eggleston) to 122 (in Willson). Of the 301 different names, 11 are common to all of the twenty-two books. In the following lists, these names are divided into two groups, (a) names of persons associated primarily with the affairs of civil life, and (b) names of persons associated primarily with military and naval affairs  Two names—those of Washington and Clinton—appear under both heads [2]

[1] Montgomery's text was not included in this computation as the copy used in the analysis of topics was not available when the enumeration of names was undertaken

[2] The validity of employing frequency of reference as a basis for determining the relative importance of different persons will be discussed in a later section  (See Section XIV)  It may be noted at this point, however, that an attempt to "equate" achievements in *different fields* upon this basis is subject to innumerable difficulties

Names common to all of the twenty-two texts; (the order is that of frequency of reference, Washington in military affairs and Franklin in civil life are each given the arbitrary value, 100):

| a)  Civil life | | b)  Military and Naval affairs | |
|---|---|---|---|
| FRANKLIN | 100 | WASHINGTON | 100 |
| PATRICK HENRY | 60 | CORNWALLIS | 42 |
| WASHINGTON | 22 | HOWE (GENERAL) | 30 |
| CLINTON | 4 | ARNOLD | 28 |
| | | CLINTON | 26 |
| | | BURGOYNE | 24 |
| | | GREENE | 20 |
| | | LAFAYETTE | 10 |
| | | GAGE | 10 |

Additional names found in at least three fourths of the books:

| a)  Civil life (FRANKLIN, 100) | | b)  Military and Naval affairs (WASHINGTON, 100) | |
|---|---|---|---|
| SAMUEL ADAMS | 63 | SCHUYLER | 15 |
| JEFFERSON | 60 | GATES | 14 |
| WILLIAM PITT | 49 | CHARLES LEE | 8 |
| JAMES OTIS | 32 | MORGAN | 8 |
| R. H. LEE | 26 | ANDRÉ | 8 |
| GEORGE III | 9 | LINCOLN | 8 |
| | | SULLIVAN | 6 |
| | | JOHN PAUL JONES | 6 |
| | | MONTGOMERY | 6 |
| | | MARION | 5 |
| | | SUMTER | 5 |
| | | WAYNE | 5 |
| | | TARLETON | 5 |
| | | PUTNAM | 4 |
| | | HOWE (ADMIRAL) | 4 |
| | | PRESCOTT | 3 |
| | | PULASKI | 3 |
| | | STARK | 3 |
| | | DE KALB | 3 |
| | | ETHAN ALLEN | 3 |
| | | PICKENS | 3 |

Additional names found in at least one half of the books

| *a) Civil life* | | *b) Military and Naval affairs* | |
|---|---|---|---|
| John Adams | 63 | George Rogers Clark | 7 |
| John Hancock | 41 | D'Estaing | 7 |
| Robert Morris | 33 | St. Leger | 5 |
| Lord North | 28 | "Lighthorse Harry" Lee | 3 |
| | | Rawdon | 3 |
| | | Steuben | 3 |
| | | Ferguson | 3 |
| | | Putnam | 3 |
| | | Tryon | 3 |
| | | DeGrasse | 3 |
| | | Rochambeau | 3 |
| | | Baum | 2 |
| | | Herkimer | 2 |
| | | Moultrie | 2 |
| | | Kosciusko | 1 |

## X

## 1783-1812

It is in the treatment of this important period that the most noticeable shifts in emphasis have occurred in the course of the four periods of publication  The following list of larger topics indicates some of these shifts of emphasis, but a consideration of the detailed topics is essential to an understanding of the more significant tendencies.

### Table XIV

| Larger Topics | Average per cent of total space of book for each of the four publication-periods | | | |
|---|---|---|---|---|
| | I | II | III | IV |
| Social and political conditions, 1783-1789 | 0 95 | 1 27 | 1 57 | 5 64 |
| Early governmental activities | 1 78 | 1.75 | 0 98 | 1 30 |
| Washington's administrations | 2 35 | 2 27 | 1.63 | 2 72 |
| Adams's administration | 0 65 | 0 90 | 0 64 | 1 14 |
| Jefferson's administrations | 1 71 | 1 65 | 1 59 | 2 18 |
| Madison's administration to the War of 1812 | 0 42 | 1.83 | 0 48 | 0 24 |
| Growth of the country, 1789-1812. | 0 22 | 0 90 | 0 66 | 1 67 |

The remarkable increase in emphasis is in connection with the first large topic,—social and political conditions between 1783 and 1789, with particular reference to the events that led to the adoption of the Constitution, the Constitutional convention, and the nature and provisions of the Constitution.

With this difference in the standards between the later textbook writers and the authors of the earlier books, it is not surprising that very few topics are common to all of the books. In fact, only two topics are found in all of the texts; these are the first two listed in the following table.

TABLE XV

| Topics common to at least 75% of the books | I | II | III | IV |
|---|---|---|---|---|
| First presidential election | 0.09 | 0.08 | 0.08 | 0.11 |
| Embargo act | 0.21 | 0.21 | 0.14 | 0.15 |
| Foreign and domestic problems under Confederation | 0.24 | 0.24 | 0.34 | 0.37 |
| Constitutional convention | 0.31 | 0.09 | 0.28 | 0.60 |
| Adoption and ratification of the Constitution | 0.30 | 0.25 | 0.36 | 0.90 |
| Washington's inauguration | 0.22 | 0.13 | 0.14 | 0.10 |
| Formation of cabinet | 0.12 | 0.05 | 0.10 | 0.18 |
| National bank and currency issue | 0.05 | 0.04 | 0.09 | 0.17 |
| Rise of political parties | 0.16 | 0.40 | 0.16 | 0.38 |
| The new capital city | 0.27 | 0.25 | 0.07 | 0.14 |
| Indian troubles | 0.30 | 0.32 | 0.13 | 0.16 |
| Relations with France (Washington's administration) | 0.18 | 0.13 | 0.12 | 0.20 |
| Jay's treaty | 0.31 | 0.25 | 0.16 | 0.23 |
| Relations with France (Adams's administration) | 0.35 | 0.29 | 0.17 | 0.27 |
| Alien and sedition acts | 0.15 | 0.16 | 0.18 | 0.22 |
| Relations with England (Jefferson's administration) | 0.15 | 0.16 | 0.21 | 0.16 |
| Louisiana Purchase | 0.15 | 0.24 | 0.23 | 0.39 |
| Chesapeake affair | 0.21 | 0.17 | 0.12 | 0.13 |
| Burr and Hamilton | 0.09 | 0.10 | 0.09 | 0.10 |
| Burr's conspiracy | 0.16 | 0.13 | 0.07 | 0.17 |
| Invention of steamboat | 0.08 | 0.10 | 0.17 | 0.18 |

| Topics common to 50%-74% of the books | I | II | III | IV |
|---|---|---|---|---|
| Articles of Confederation | 0.22 | 0.25 | 0.13 | 0.51 |
| The Confederation | 0.24 | 0.00 | 0.18 | 0.35 |
| Problems of individual states | 0.09 | 0.22 | 0.20 | 0.32 |
| Features of the Constitution | 0.05 | 0.79 | 0.28 | 2.71 |
| Shays's rebellion | 0.18 | 0.07 | 0.07 | 0.09 |
| Systems of revenue | 0.08 | 0.00 | 0.08 | 0.14 |
| New states (Washington's administration) | 0.25 | 0.00 | 0.17 | 0.17 |
| Whisky rebellion | 0.12 | 0.09 | 0.12 | 0.17 |
| Relations with England (Washington's adm.) | 0.18 | 0.18 | 0.08 | 0.15 |
| Genet affair | 0.11 | 0.14 | 0.14 | 0.11 |
| Relations with Spain | 0.08 | 0.13 | 0.07 | 0.12 |
| Farewell address | 0.09 | 0.20 | 0.15 | 0.16 |
| Election, 1796 | 0.11 | 0.09 | 0.09 | 0.12 |
| Election, 1800 | 0.19 | 0.12 | 0.18 | 0.18 |
| War with France | 0.15 | 0.08 | 0.08 | 0.17 |
| New states (Adams's administration) | 0.15 | 0.00 | 0.10 | 0.06 |
| Lewis and Clark | 0.00 | 0.13 | 0.29 | 0.24 |
| Barbary States treaties | 0.00 | 0.29 | 0.20 | 0.18 |
| War with Barbary States | 0.50 | 0.23 | 0.00 | 0.17 |
| Impressment | 0.13 | 0.32 | 0.10 | 0.09 |
| Non-intercourse act | 0.09 | 0.30 | 0.07 | 0.12 |
| Westward expansion | 0.07 | 1.10 | 0.23 | 0.37 |
| Ordinance of 1787 | 0.03 | 0.00 | 0.11 | 0.23 |

The above table indicates the specific topics that have been given increased emphasis in the books of Class III and Class IV. The most notable increase is in the discussion of the Constitution, but attention may also be called to the larger proportion of space devoted to the Articles of Confederation, the Ordinance of 1787, the Lewis and Clark expedition, the currency problem, the treatment of foreign relations, and the introduction of steam navigation.

In respect of number of names mentioned, the range is from 22 in Ellis to 95 in Woodburn and Moran. The median book contains 37 names. Common to all of the books are five names. The order is based upon frequency of reference; (for every 100 references to Washington, there are 88 to Jefferson, etc.)

| | | | |
|---|---|---|---|
| WASHINGTON | 100 | JOHN ADAMS | 42 |
| JEFFERSON | 88 | MADISON | 35 |
| HAMILTON | 53 | | |

Three additional names are found in 22 out of the 23 books used in this phase of the analysis [1]

(WASHINGTON, 100)

| | |
|---|---|
| AARON BURR | 20 |
| JOHN JAY | 18 |
| NAPOLEON I | 18 |

The following additional names are common to at least three fourths of the books: (Washington, 100)

| | | | |
|---|---|---|---|
| CHARLES C. PINCKNEY | 13 | ROBERT FULTON | 6 |
| BENJAMIN FRANKLIN | 10 | TECUMSEH | 6 |
| "CITIZEN" GENET | 9 | DANIEL SHAYS | 5 |
| WILLIAM CLARK | 9 | W. H HARRISON | 4 |
| JOHN MARSHALL | 9 | HENRY KNOX | 4 |
| MERIWETHER LEWIS | 9 | | |

In at least one half of the books additional names are found as follows. (Washington, 100).

| | | | |
|---|---|---|---|
| ELI WHITNEY | 7 | EDMUND RANDOLPH | 4 |
| ANTHONY WAYNE | 5 | HENRY CLAY | 4 |
| GEORGE CLINTON | 5 | ARTHUR ST CLAIR. | 3 |
| R R LIVINGSTON | 5 | ROBERT MORRIS | 3 |
| JAMES MONROE | 5 | ELBRIDGE GERRY | 3 |
| STEPHEN DECATUR | 4 | PATRICK HENRY | 3 |

[1] Two texts used in the topical analysis (Montgomery and Goodrich) were not available when these determinations were made The texts of Gordy and Dickson replaced them

## XI

### 1812-1861

For convenience in dealing with this long and important period. the analysis of specific topics is presented under six large heads   The average proportions of space devoted to these large heads during the four publication-periods are shown in the following table:

TABLE XVI

| Larger Topics | Average per cent of total space of book for each of the four publication-periods | | | |
|---|---|---|---|---|
| | I | II | III | IV |
| War of 1812 .. . .. ... ..      .    .. .. | 6 06 | 3 22 | 3 40 | 3 00 |
| War with Mexico . .. ... ... ... .. ... .. ... | 3 46 | 1 87 | 1.54 | 1 49 |
| Political affairs, including slavery problems .. .. .. .. .. ... .. .. ... .. .. ... | 3 40 | 2 48 | 4 13 | 5 41 |
| Industry, invention, and commerce.... .. .. | 0 35 | 0 68 | 1 73 | 2 31 |
| Foreign affairs . ... . . .. .. .. .. | 0.10 | 0.30 | 0 67 | 0 99 |
| Finance ......... ... ............. .. .......... ... .. ..... | 0 60 | 0 42 | 0.67 | 1 00 |
| Territorial growth .     .. .. . .  .. . | 0 60 | 2.48 | 1 84 | 1 37 |

Some of the tendencies noted in the treatment of the preceding periods are clearly in evidence here, particularly the decreasing proportion of space devoted to wars   Very significant, too, is the striking increase in the attention that is given to industry and commerce, to foreign affairs, and to financial problems.

The distribution of emphasis among the more specific topics under the first two heads is shown in the following table

TABLE XVII

A   THE WAR OF 1812

| Topics common to all books | Publication-periods | | | | Topics common to 75% 99% of the books | Publication-periods | | | |
|---|---|---|---|---|---|---|---|---|---|
| | I | II | III | IV | | I | II | III | IV |
| Causes   .  . | 0 12 | 0 35 | 0 85 | 1 03 | Hartford Convention | 0 20 | 0 10 | 0 21 | 0 17 |
| Naval battles . . . . . | 1 86 | 0 73 | 0 62 | 0 66 | | | | | |
| Detroit and Washington  . . . .  . .. | 0 38 | 0 29 | 0 23 | 0 21 | | | | | |
| New Orleans . ... . | 0 29 | 0.17 | 0 17 | 0 18 | | | | | |
| Treaty of Ghent   . | 0 13 | 0 08 | 0 28 | 0 21 | | | | | |

B   THE WAR WITH MEXICO

| | I | II | III | IV |
|---|---|---|---|---|
| Causes  ..     . ..| 0 19 | 0 15 | 0 23 | 0 23 |
| Buena Vista   .    . | 0 16 | 0 14 | 0 15 | 0 08 |
| Vera Cruz, Cerro Gordo . . . | 0 30 | 0 15 | 0 18 | 0 06 |
| Capture of City of Mexico . . | 0 44 | 0 31 | 0 21 | 0 09 |
| Monterey and California .  . ... . _  .. | 0 44 | 0 16 | 0 23 | 0 16 |
| Treaty and results of war  ..     . . | 0.16 | 0 10 | 0 13 | 0 09 |

The tendencies in the treatment of military campaigns and especially of specific engagements are clearly shown in the above table The proportion of space devoted to the naval battles of the War of 1812 has shrunk to about one third of its former dimensions; Buena Vista has lost just one half of its earlier significance; Vera Cruz and Cerro Gordo are apparently but one fifth as important as in the earlier books; and the significance of the capture of the City of Mexico has declined in about the same proportion. On the other hand much heavier emphasis is being given to the causes of the wars, and especially to the causes of the War of 1812. The decline in the attention given to the results of the War with Mexico is, however, more difficult to justify.

The specific topics relating to the third large head,—political affairs,—are listed in the following table which is presented in three parts,—the first comprising the topics common to all of the books, the second, comprising the topics common to at least three fourths of the books and the third comprising the topics common to at least one half of the books.

TABLE XVIII

POLITICAL AFFAIRS, INCLUDING SLAVERY PROBLEMS

| Topics common to all books | Publication-periods | | | |
| --- | --- | --- | --- | --- |
| | I | II | III | IV |
| Causes of friction between the northern and southern states .... ... .. .. .... ... .. .. .. .. | 0 16 | 0 19 | 0 36 | 0 36 |
| Missouri Compromise .. ..... .... ............. ... ... .... | 0 10 | 0 16 | 0 18 | 0 25 |
| California and the Compromise of 1850 ... .... | 0 14 | 0 27 | 0 39 | 0 37 |
| Fugitive-slave law ............ ... ..... .. .. .. .. | 0 05 | 0 13 | 0 25 | 0 15 |
| Kansas-Nebraska act and associated events.. | 0 31 | 0 25 | 0 55 | 0 66 |
| John Brown's raid ... .. .. .. ..... .. .. . .. .. .. | 0 31 | 0.10 | 0.30 | 0 32 |

| Topics common to 75% 99% of the books | Publication-periods | | | | Topics common to 50%-74% of the books | Publication periods | | | |
| --- | --- | --- | --- | --- | --- | --- | --- | --- | --- |
| | I | II | III | IV | | I | II | III | IV |
| Work and influence of the Abolitionists .... .0.05 | 0.05 | 0 04 | 0 13 | 0 20 | Lincoln-Douglas debates ..... | 0 00 | 0 00 | 0 21 | 0 24 |
| Wilmot proviso .. . | 0 10 | 0 15 | 0 12 | 0 15 | Work of W L Garrison . ... | 0 05 | 0 00 | 0 11 | 0 11 |
| Texan independence and admission .. | 0 08 | 0 14 | 0 21 | 0 10 | | | | | |
| Dred Scott decision . | 0 09 | 0.16 | 0 25 | 0 24 | | | | | |

The significant increases in emphasis are in connection with the compromises of 1820 and 1850, the events associated with Kansas and Nebraska, and the Dred Scott decision The complete neglect of the Lincoln-Douglas debates in the textbooks of the first two publication periods perhaps illustrates the difficulty that those who are close to an event in point of time necessarily experience in gauging its real significance.

Table XVIII presents the topics common to at least three fourths and to at least one half of the books in connection with industry and commerce during this period   There are no topics that are common to all of the books.

TABLE XIX

INVENTION, INDUSTRY, AND COMMERCE

| Topics common to 75%-99% of the books | Publication periods | | | | Topics common to 50%-74% of the books | Publication periods | | | |
|---|---|---|---|---|---|---|---|---|---|
| | I | II | III | IV | | I | II | III | IV |
| Canal development . | 0 02 | 0 10 | 0 23 | 0 24 | Mining development, especially gold and silver ... ... .. | 0 05 | 0 09 | 0 11 | 0 11 |
| Tariff dicussion and legislation . | 0 22 | 0 15 | 0 26 | 0 41 | Development of manufacturing .... | 0 04 | 0 02 | 0 16 | 0 14 |
| Railroads and related topics ..... . | 0 00 | 0 15 | 0 31 | 0 34 | | | | | |
| Telegraph | 0 03 | 0 07 | 0 15 | 0 16 | | | | | |
| Other inventions | 0 02 | 0 05 | 0 21 | 0 52 | | | | | |

It is noticeable that the movement toward a more adequate recognition of commercial and industrial development as important topics in elementary history began in the second publication-period (1881-1888) and is clearly marked in the third publication-period (1892-1904)   The increased attention given to tariff legislation by the most recent books is also significant.

In connection with the fourth large head,—foreign affairs,—there are no topics common to all of the books.  In at least three fourths of the books, the following topics are found:

TABLE XX

FOREIGN AFFAIRS

| Topics common to 75%-99% of the books | Average per cent of entire space of book for each of the four publication-periods | | | |
|---|---|---|---|---|
| | I | II | III | IV |
| Monroe doctrine and related events. . | 0 12 | 0 24 | 0 24 | 0 25 |
| European events involved in American problems .. .. .. .. .. .. .. .. .. .. | 0 00 | 0 07 | 0 18 | 0 23 |

Table XXI presents the topics common to all books and the topics common to three fourths of the books under the last two large heads.— finance and territorial growth.

TABLE XXI

FINANCE

| Topics common to all books | Publication periods | | | | Topics common to 75%-99% of the books | Publication-periods | | | |
|---|---|---|---|---|---|---|---|---|---|
| | I | II | III | IV | | I | II | III | IV |
| United States bank issue | 0 31 | 0 14 | 0 36 | 0 45 | Financial panics | 0 13 | 0 24 | 0 24 | 0 25 |
| Tariff discussion and legislation   .... | 0 22 | 0 15 | 0 26 | 0 41 | Currency bills | 0 27 | 0 03 | 0 11 | 0 10 |

TERRITORIAL GROWTH

| Topics common to all books | Publication periods | | | | Topics common to 75%-99% of the books | Publication periods | | | |
|---|---|---|---|---|---|---|---|---|---|
| | I | II | III | IV | | I | II | III | IV |
| Admission of new states .. | 0 30 | 1 71 | 0 32 | 0 18 | Territorial accessions resulting from Mexican war . . | 0 08 | 0 08 | 0 10 | 0 09 |
| | | | | | Florida . . . . | 0 05 | 0 11 | 0 11 | 0 12 |
| | | | | | Oregon country | 0 16 | 0 31 | 0 20 | 0 71 |
| | | | | | Settlement of the West. | 0 10 | 0 19 | 0 62 | 0 44 |

Several interesting and perhaps significant facts are revealed by these two tables· the very heavy emphasis that was given to the admission of new states in the books of the second publication-period (1881-1888), the increased attention to the national-bank controversy and the financial panics; the generally increased attention given to the settlement of the West during the last two publication-periods, and to the Oregon country in the most recent books.

The number of different names mentioned in connection with this period is surprisingly large,— four hundred ninety-nine  The average books contains 112 different names and the median book, 101.  The range is from 55 (in Eggleston) to 185 (in Shinn).

Of the 499 different names mentioned, only 15 are common to all of the books,—and nine of these are the names of presidents, leaving six persons not presidents whose names appear in all of the books  The common names are the following; the order again is that of frequency:

| a) Civil life | | b) Military and Naval Affairs | |
|---|---|---|---|
| ANDREW JACKSON .. .. .. .. | 100 | TAYLOR . .. .. .. . .. .. .. .. | 100 |
| CLAY ... .... .. .. .... .. . .. .. .. | 86 | SCOTT ... .. . .. .. . . .. | 80 |
| JOHN QUINCY ADAMS . ... .. .. .. | 77 | JACKSON .. .. .. .. ... .. .. .. .. | 68 |
| VAN BUREN .. .. .. . . . .. | 56 | HARRISON . . . .. .. .... . | 59 |
| MONROE .. .. .... . .. .... .. .. . | 54 | KEARNY . . . .. ... . .. . | 40 |
| MADISON . .. .. . .. .. | 45 | SANTA ANNA .. ..... .. ...... .. .. .. | 39 |
| TYLER ... ... .. .. .. .. ... .. .. | 45 | FREMONT .. ... .. .. . .. . . | 18 |
| POLK . . . .. .. .... .. .. .. .. | 42 | | |
| TAYLOR . . . .. . .. | 40 | | |
| HARRISON . . . .... .. .. .. | 33 | | |
| SCOTT . . . . .. . . .. .. .. .. | 30 | | |
| FREMONT . .. . .. .. .. | 30 | | |

The following names are found in at least three fourths of the books:

| a) Civil life (JACKSON, 100) | | b) Military and Naval Affairs (TAYLOR, 100) | |
|---|---|---|---|
| LINCOLN . | 57 | O H PERRY | 44 |
| WEBSTER . | 51 | TECUMSEH | 42 |
| CALHOUN | 49 | LAWRENCE | 24 |
| DOUGLAS . | 44 | HULL (GENERAL) | 23 |
| BUCHANAN | 37 | ISAAC HULL | 18 |
| JEFFERSON | 33 | McDONOUGH | 17 |
| PIERCE . | 28 | DORR | 13 |
| FILLMORE | 24 | | |
| WASHINGTON . | 22 | | |
| JOHN BROWN . | 17 | | |
| S F. B MORSE | 16 | | |
| LaFAYETTE | 13 | | |

The following additional names are found in at least one half of the books:

| a) Civil life (JACKSON, 100) | | b) Military and Naval Affairs (TAYLOR, 100) | |
|---|---|---|---|
| W. L. GARRISON | 18 | PROCTOR | 67 |
| SUMNER | 13 | NAPOLEON I | 61 |
| DRED SCOTT | 13 | H. DEARBORN . | 18 |
| JOHN ADAMS | 12 | JACOB BROWN | 17 |
| ROBERT HAYNE . | 11 | SIR ISAAC BROCK | 16 |
| JOSEPH SMITH | 11 | OSCEOLA | 16 |
| DE WITT CLINTON | 11 | PAKENHAM | 16 |
| M C PERRY | 10 | DECATUR | 12 |
| W H. SEWARD | 10 | SOLOMON VAN RENSSELAER | 10 |
| J. C. BRECKENRIDGE | 10 | STOCKTON | 9 |
| W. H. CRAWFORD . | 9 | SLOAT | 9 |
| JEFFERSON DAVIS . | 9 | BLACKHAWK | 8 |
| LORD ASHBURTON | 8 | | |
| LEWIS CASS . | 7 | | |
| DAVID WILMOT | 7 | | |
| JOHN BELL . | 6 | | |
| CYRUS McCORMICK | 6 | | |
| A. H STEPHENS . | 6 | | |
| BLACKHAWK | 6 | | |
| BRIGHAM YOUNG | 5 | | |

## XII

## THE CIVIL WAR

The proportion of space to the Civil war has fallen rather consistently and steadily since the first publication period,—from 18 8% in books of Class I to 10.22% in books of Class IV  The "common topics" are naturally numerous here; the following table indicates the topics common to all of the books.

TABLE XXII

| Topics common to all books | Average per cent of space of entire book in each of the four publication-periods | | | |
|---|---|---|---|---|
| | I | II | III | IV |
| Fort Sumter and events immediately associated | 0 72 | 0 31 | 0 21 | 0 20 |
| Bull Run | 0 36 | 0 22 | 0 30 | 0 30 |
| Trent affair | 0 28 | 0 18 | 0 16 | 0 20 |
| The blockade | 0 25 | 0 14 | 0 19 | 0 18 |
| Peninsular campaign | 0.70 | 0 85 | 0 47 | 0 44 |
| Forts Henry and Donelson | 0 19 | 0 24 | 0 19 | 0 18 |
| Shiloh | 0 27 | 0 29 | 0 14 | 0 25 |
| New Orleans | 0 41 | 0 43 | 0 22 | 0 13 |
| Antietam | 0 08 | 0 15 | 0 10 | 0 12 |
| Merrimac and Monitor | 0 49 | 0 70 | 0 42 | 0 38 |
| Fredericksburg | 0 08 | 0 12 | 0 06 | 0 12 |
| Emancipation proclamation | 0 13 | 0 39 | 0 12 | 0 13 |
| Chancellorsville | 0 11 | 0 13 | 0 13 | 0 14 |
| Gettysburg | 0 13 | 0 28 | 0 56 | 0 31 |
| Vicksburg | 0 30 | 0 43 | 0 41 | 0 22 |
| Chickamauga | 0 10 | 0 18 | 0 14 | 0 12 |
| Battles around Chattanooga | 0.17 | 0 50 | 0 25 | 0 13 |
| The Wilderness campaign | 0.17 | 0 35 | 0 19 | 0 20 |
| Atlanta and Sherman's march | 0 32 | 0 32 | 0 18 | 0 19 |
| Early's raid | 0 15 | 0 11 | 0 13 | 0 11 |
| Sheridan's campaign | 0 21 | 0 24 | 0 16 | 0 12 |
| Fall of Richmond | 0 17 | 0 32 | 0 12 | 0 13 |
| Appomattox | 0 95 | 0 17 | 0 14 | 0 17 |
| Assassination of Lincoln | 0 19 | 0 27 | 0 11 | 0 24 |

The topical analysis made for the period of the Civil war was less detailed than that made for the other periods, consequently topics common to three fourths and to one half of the books cannot be presented  In the report of the collaborator to whom this period was assigned, the following additional topics are listed as "frequently mentioned".

The Baltimore incident (infrequent in the recent books)
Contest for Missouri
Roanoke Island
Kentucky campaign
Fort Fisher
Murfreesboro
Mobile Bay
Nashville
Morgan's raid
Admission of West Virginia
New York draft riots

The total number of different names mentioned in all of these books for the Civil-war period was not determined. The median book contains 67 different names, and the range is from 132 (Willson) to 35 (Dickson) and 38 (Turpin) Nineteen names are found in all of the books. The detail in which the campaigns are treated makes "frequency of reference" an untrustworthy index of the relative emphasis which the textbook writers give to the various names The following groupings, however, may be somewhat suggestive of this emphasis the "weights" are based upon the average number of times each name is mentioned

### NAMES FOUND IN ALL BOOKS

| Non-Military | | Military and Naval | |
|---|---|---|---|
| LINCOLN | 100 | LEE | 100 |
| DAVIS | 16 | GRANT | 91 |
| | | SHERMAN | 58 |
| | | McCLELLAN | 49 |
| | | J E. JOHNSTON | 38 |
| | | T J JACKSON | 25 |
| | | G. H THOMAS | 22 |
| | | P H SHERIDAN | 20 |
| | | J. HOOKER | 19 |
| | | W S ROSECRANS | 16 |
| | | D G FARRAGUT | 16 |
| | | J. EARLY | 15 |
| | | D C BUELL | 13 |
| | | G H MEADE | 13 |
| | | A. E. BURNSIDE | 12 |
| | | I McDOWELL | 12 |
| | | R ANDERSON | 8 |

ADDITIONAL NAMES FOUND IN ALL BOOKS EXCEPT ONE

| *Non-Military* (LINCOLN, 100) | | *Military and Naval* (LEE, 100) | |
|---|---|---|---|
| J. M MASON | 7 | B BRAGG | 28 |
| J. SLIDELL | 7 | J B HOOD | 20 |
| | | P G. T BEAUREGARD | 11 |

ADDITIONAL NAMES FOUND IN AT LEAST THREE FOURTHS OF THE BOOKS

| *Non-Military* (LINCOLN, 100) | | *Military and Naval* (LEE, 100) | |
|---|---|---|---|
| J. ERICSSON | 5 | J POPE | 12 |
| | | B BUTLER | 9 |
| | | N. P. BANKS | 8 |
| | | A S JOHNSTON | 7 |
| | | J C. PEMBERTON | 6 |
| | | H W HALLECK | 6 |
| | | J C. FREMONT | 5 |
| | | A H FOOTE | 5 |
| | | W SCOTT | 5 |
| | | C WILKES | 4 |

ADDITIONAL NAMES FOUND IN AT LEAST ONE HALF OF THE BOOKS

| *Non-Military* (LINCOLN, 100) | | *Military and Naval* (LEE, 100) | |
|---|---|---|---|
| A. JOHNSON | 5 | J. LONGSTREET | 7 |
| W H SEWARD | 5 | D D PORTER | 5 |
| J. W BOOTH | 3 | G E PICKETT | 4 |
| | | J M SCHOFIELD | 4 |
| | | E VAN DORN | 4 |
| | | N. LYON | 3 |
| | | R SEMMES | 3 |

# XIII

## 1865-1912

This period is naturally difficult to treat satisfactorily  The books of Class I mention only the events immediately following the close of the Civil war, and the emphasis given by the later books to the more recent events is extremely variable.  In addition to a greatly increased emphasis upon reconstruction, few distinct tendencies are to be noted in the following table showing the proportion of space devoted to the larger topics in the books of the four publication periods

TABLE XXIII

| Large Topics | Average per cent of space of entire book devoted to each topic in the four publication-periods | | | |
|---|---|---|---|---|
| | I | II[1] | III | IV |
| Reconstruction | 1.11 | 0 67 | 1 50 | 6 06 |
| National legislation | 0 21 | 1 05 | 1 29 | 1 63 |
| Federal activities in regulation, control, and defense | 0 23 | 0 35 | 0 83 | 1 11 |
| Political parties | 0 93 | 1.62 | 1.31 | 1.55 |
| Indian affairs | 0 00 | 0 73 | 0 29 | 0 12 |
| Great disasters | 0 08 | 0 58 | 0 43 | 0 22 |
| Commercial and industrial development | 0.29 | 0 98 | 1 39 | 0 93 |
| Labor problems | 0 00 | 0.69 | 0 67 | 0.25 |
| Social progress (including education) | 0 00 | 0 04 | 0.23 | 0.08 |
| Conservation movements | 0 00 | 0.00 | 0 45 | 0 33 |
| Territorial expansion | 0 00 | 0 12 | 0 43 | 0 42 |
| Foreign relations | 0 46 | 1.18 | 0 78 | 1 00 |
| War with Spain | 0.00 | 0.71 | 1.58 | 1 62 |
| Miscellaneous items | 0 21 | 0 25 | 0 36 | 0 19 |

[1]In some of the books assigned to this publication period, the edition used in the study included material added to the earlier editions.

No significant topic except the reference to the beginning of Johnson's administration is common to all of the books. The following table includes the topics common to at least three fourths and at least one half of the books:

TABLE XXIV

| Topics common to 75%-99% of the books | Publication-periods | | | |
|---|---|---|---|---|
| | I | II | III | IV |
| Conflict between Congress and President Johnson | 0 45 | 0 11 | 0 10 | 0 19 |
| Impeachment of Johnson | 0 39 | 0.10 | 0 12 | 0 08 |
| 14th Amendment | 0 08 | 0 05 | 0 08 | 0 15 |
| 15th Amendment | 0 12 | 0 06 | 0 04 | 0 07 |
| Admission of new states | 0 14 | 0 25 | 0 14 | 0 18 |
| Electoral commission | 0 23 | 0 08 | 0 15 | 0 10 |
| Presidential campaigns and elections | 0 18 | 1 18 | 0 80 | 1 05 |
| Assination of Garfield and McKinley | 0 34 | 0 23 | 0 22 | 0 15 |

| Topics common to 50%-74% of the books | Publication periods | | | |
|---|---|---|---|---|
| | I | II | III | IV |
| Policy of Johnson | 0 23 | 0 11 | 0 14 | 0 12 |
| Policy of Congress | 0 00 | 0 05 | 0 12 | 0 27 |
| Military rule in the South | 0 00 | 0 10 | 0 22 | 0 20 |
| Carpet baggers | 0 00 | 0 04 | 0 16 | 0 21 |
| Restoration of seceded states | 0 00 | 0 04 | 0 08 | 0 06 |
| Specie-payments | 0 00 | 0 00 | 0 17 | 0 11 |
| Bland-Allison act | 0 00 | 0 08 | 0 07 | 0 09 |
| Repeal of silver purchase act | 0 00 | 0 16 | 0 08 | 0 09 |
| 13th Amendment | 0 00 | 0 05 | 0 06 | 0 08 |
| Indian affairs | 0 00 | 0 73 | 0 29 | 0 12 |
| Alaska purchase | 0 00 | 0 10 | 0 09 | 0 10 |
| Northwestern boundaries | 0 00 | 0 11 | 0 09 | 0 09 |
| Alabama claims | 0 46 | 0 18 | 0 15 | 0 11 |

| | | | |
|---|---|---|---|
| Transcontinental rail-road . .. | 0 00 | 0 17 | 0 22 | 0 15 |
| Financial crises | 0 00 | 0 28 | 0 27 | 0 18 |
| Expositions .. . | 0 46 | 0 76 | 0 49 | 0 31 |
| Great fires .. | . 0 08 | 0 26 | 0 12 | 0 08 |
| Strikes, riots, etc . | 0 00 | 0 58 | 0 46 | 0 18 |
| Fisheries disputes .. | 0 00 | 0 16 | 0 15 | 0 15 |
| Rise of new political parties | 0 41 | 0 16 | 0 21 | 0 20 |
| Opening reservation lands . | . 0 00 | 0 06 | 0 25 | 0 12 |
| Civil service reform . | 0 00 | 0 08 | 0 13 | 0 18 |
| Australian ballot | 0 00 | 0 11 | 0 09 | 0 09 |
| Chinese exclusion act | 0 00 | 0 31 | 0 09 | 0 10 |
| Presidential succession law . ... | . 0 00 | 0 12 | 0 08 | 0 10 |
| Interstate commerce act .. . ... . | . 0 00 | 0 03 | 0 06 | 0 10 |
| Venezuelan episode.. | .0 00 | 0 00 | 0 11 | 0 12 |
| McKinley tariff | . 0 00 | 0 11 | 0 07 | 0 11 |
| Wilson tariff .. | 0 00 | 0 08 | 0 07 | 0 08 |
| Cuban revolution .. | 0 00 | 0 14 | 0 15 | 0 14 |
| The "Maine" .. | 0 00 | 0 07 | 0 13 | 0 12 |
| Spanish war—preliminary activities . . ... | 0 00 | 0 00 | 0 26 | 0 23 |
| Manila Bay .... | 0 00 | 0 10 | 0 18 | 0 21 |
| Cuban campaign and defeat of Spanish fleet ... . . .. | .0 00 | 0 20 | 0 24 | 0 40 |
| Porto Rican campaign | 0 00 | 0 03 | 0 19 | 0 25 |
| Treaty of peace .. ... | .0 00 | 0 09 | 0 08 | 0 13 |
| Administration of new colonies .. . . ... | . 0 00 | 0 21 | 0 26 | 0 29 |
| Panama canal . . .. | .0.00 | 0 27 | 0 23 | 0 30 |

The difficulty of determining the historical significance of con-temporary or very recent events is clearly revealed in the above table. In order to meet the demands of the "market," the writer of a text-book in elementary history will bring his treatment as nearly "up to date" as possible  Every textbook, then, is liable to misplacements of emphasis in dealing with the events immediately preceding its pub-lication.  The heavy emphasis upon Indian troubles in the books of the second publication-period is a case in point  The attention given to great fires, to financial panics, and to expositions is also likely to decline as these events recede in time.  On the other hand, there are certain events which grow in importance as the years reveal their in-fluence; the details of the reconstruction days in the South as con-trasted with the legislation of reconstruction may be cited as an in-stance

One hundred eighty-two different names are found relating to this period.  The name of President Johnson is the only one common to all the books  At least three fourths of the books mention the fol-lowing names (the order is based upon the average number of times mentioned, but "weights" are not given in view of the relative recency of most of the events connected with the names) .

| | |
|---|---|
| JOHNSON | HARRISON |
| McKINLEY | ARTHUR |
| CLEVELAND | BLAINE |
| GRANT | TILDEN |
| DEWEY | GREELEY |
| LINCOLN | |

At least one half of the books contain the following eighteen names (the order again is based upon frequency of mention):

| | |
|---|---|
| CERVERA | SHAFTER |
| ROOSEVELT | SCHLEY |
| JOHN SHERMAN | CUSTER |
| SAMPSON | W A WHEELER |
| MAXIMILIAN | HENDRICKS |
| HOBSON | HANCOCK |
| H. WILSON | N. A MILES |
| CYRUS W FIELD | A E STEVENSON |
| STANTON | |

Only 31 names are common to at least half of books as against 46, the number in the median book.

## XIV

## THE 'HALL OF FAME"

The significance of the elementary history taught in the seventh and eighth grades is due in part, as we have said, to the fact that it is the initial, *systematic* study of the subject that is undertaken in most of our schools. But elementary history is significant for at least two additional reasons  in the first place, it supplies a core of common information to a very large proportion of the individuals who will make up the next generation; and, in the second place, it supplies this information at a period of life when ideals are readily formed, and especially ideals that cluster about personalities

For all of these reasons, the *names* that recur in the pages of these elementary textbooks are of fundamental import    There is no other "Hall of Fame" that can compare with the elementary text-book in national history in keeping alive the memories of those who have gone before. Whether this is a function that elementary education *should* discharge is a question that does not concern us just now; it is a fact that elementary history constitutes a "Hall of Fame," and it is well to know to what characters it is insuring a relatively high measure of immortality.

The names that are most frequently mentioned in the treatment of each of the periods of our national history are listed in the preceding pages  In considering the periods from the close of the French and Indian war to the close of the Civil war, an attempt was made to deter-mine the relative significance of each name by noting the relative fre-quency of reference. The more adequate method of noting the pro-portions of space devoted to achievements was employed in connec-tion with the period of discovery and exploration, but this method could not be effectively applied to the later periods, and the standard of frequency was used as constituting the best available substitute  In fact, neither method is thoroughly satisfactory. As Johnson says  "Pages alone, of course, do not necessarily indicate the relative impor-tance attached to topics   From a recent study of the fame of Euripides as compared with the fame of Sophocles, it appears that Euripides gets the greater space in the histories, but Sophocles gets the adjectives and is therefore judged the more famous  A textbook writer may show his emphasis by his adjectives."[1]  But Johnson goes on to say, "Pages are none the less a rough test," and he would doubtless agree that frequency of reference is also a rough test. Every mention of a name increases the chances that it and the events with which it is associated

[1] H Johnson: *Teaching  f History*  p 282

will be retained and recalled; whether this frequency of reference is a trustworthy measure of the fame or infamy that a character deserves, it is at least a fairly accurate gauge of the degree in which his fame or infamy will be known to the succeeding generation

Two lists of names have been compiled from the data included in the different lists presented for each of the periods between 1765 and 1865  The names again have been separated into two groups,— one comprising the persons apparently most prominent in civil life, the other comprising the persons apparently most prominent in military and naval affairs.  This separation may not be justified; it is based upon the fact that descriptions of battles and campaigns often involve the repetition of names in close sequence, while the description of events that are primarily political, economic, or industrial in their character will not involve this repetition.  It is probably the repetition of the same name in connection with *different* events that has the largest influence in impressing the name upon the memory; hence the effect of the many repetitions in connection with single battles or campaigns may perhaps be legitimately discounted  In any case, this has been done to the extent at least of providing the two lists just mentioned.

The twenty-five persons apparently most prominent in civil life during the century, 1765-1865, are the following; (Lincoln, as the character having the highest frequency of reference, is given the value, 100; for every 100 times that Lincoln is mentioned, Washington—as a participant in civil affairs—is mentioned 84 times, Jefferson, 82 times, etc.) :

| | |
|---|---|
| LINCOLN ............ .100 | STEPHEN A. DOUGLAS ....  ..... 18 |
| *WASHINGTON .. .... ......... ... 84 | BUCHANAN ..... ...... ... 16 |
| JEFFERSON .. ... .... .. .. .. 82 | JOHN TYLER .. ... ..... 16 |
| *JACKSON . .. ..... .. ... ..... . 49 | JEFFERSON DAVIS . ...... .. 15 |
| JOHN ADAMS ..... .. ... 46 | J K POLK ........ .... 15 |
| MADISON ..... .. .. ... ...... 40 | *TAYLOR .. .... ...... .... 14 |
| HAMILTON ......... .... ..... 37 | AARON BURR . ... ...... 14 |
| HENRY CLAY .. . ...... 33 | JOHN JAY .. .. ... ... ... 12 |
| J. Q ADAMS .. .. .... . 29 | *W. H HARRISON . .. ...... 12 |
| MONROE .. ...... .. . ... .. 23 | |
| FRANKLIN .. ...... 23 | |
| PATRICK HENRY ... .. .. . .. ... 21 | |
| VAN BUREN . .... ... . ... .. 20 | |
| CALHOUN ... .. .. . .. ... .. .. 20 | |
| WEBSTER . ..... ... ... ... .... . ...... 20 | |
| SAMUEL ADAMS ... .. . ... . 18 | |

The names that are marked with an asterisk (*) are also found in the military and naval list   Their rank in this civil list is determined by the frequency of reference to these men as participants in the affairs of civil life only.

The above list includes only the Americans whose names were mentioned most frequently   The three Europeans who apparently had the largest influence upon American affairs during the century in question were the following; (Lincoln again is taken as the basis of comparison)

(LINCOLN, 100)

| | |
|---|---|
| NAPOLEON | 19 |
| GEORGE III | 19 |
| WILLIAM PITT | 12 |

School histories are frequently criticised for their failure to recognize leadership in phases of national life other than political and military.   The absence of certain names among the twenty-five most frequently mentioned does not mean that the textbooks do not mention them, but rather that the historical narrative follows chiefly the series of causes and effects represented by political development and its accompanying conflicts.   The recurrence of names is therefore most likely to be limited to these fields.   Non-political and non-military achievements which have greatly influenced the course of events have been noted with increasing emphasis in the texts of the two latest periods, but a single reference usually suffices for such names, for example, as those of Fulton, Morse, and McCormick   In so far as frequency of reference increases the chances of permanent impression and ready recall, it is highly probable that the pupil in the seventh and eighth grades is likely to gain, under the present organization of historical materials, an exaggerated idea of the importance of political and military achievement as contrasted with industrial achievement. In so far as achievement in literature and art is concerned, the danger is not so great for these fields are taken care of by other divisions of the curriculum

The persons that have apparently been most important in the military and naval affairs of the century, 1765-1865, are the following; (Washington, as the person most frequently mentioned, is given the value, 100)

| | | | |
|---|---|---|---|
| WASHINGTON | 100 | CORNWALLIS | 42 |
| R E LEE | 83 | McCLELLAN | 41 |
| GRANT | 76 | J E JOHNSTON | 32 |
| W T. SHERMAN | 48 | HOWE (GENERAL) | 30 |

| | | | |
|---|---|---|---|
| ARNOLD | 28 | J HOOKER | 16 |
| CLINTON | 26 | PHILIP SCHUYLER | 15 |
| BURGOYNE | 24 | J EARLY | 14 |
| "STONEWALL" JACKSON | 20 | GAGE | 14 |
| NATHANAEL GREENE | 20 | FARRAGUT | 13 |
| ZACHARY TAYLOR | 19 | W H HARRISON | 13 |
| WINFIELD SCOTT | 19 | ANDREW JACKSON | 13 |
| G H THOMAS | 18 | G. H MEADE | 13 |
| SHERIDAN | 17 | | |

In order to determine whether the relative emphasis given by the textbooks to different characters in our national history was abnormal as compared with the emphasis accorded to these characters in other types of books, the relative proportion of space given to the same names in the *Encyclopedia Britannica* (11th edition) was computed (but only for those apparently important in the affairs of civil life). The correlation between the two lists is represented by the Pearson coefficient 27 [1] The most notable discrepancy is in the case of Franklin who would be ranked Number 2 by the *Britannica* (instead of Number 11, his rank in the textbooks) Other significant shifts of emphasis are to be noted in connection with Washington (Number 3 instead of Number 2); Hamilton (Number 5 instead of Number 7); Clay (Number 11 instead of Number 8); John Adams (Number 16 instead of Number 5); J. Q Adams (Number 17 instead of Number 9); Patrick Henry (Number 23 instead of Number 12); Monroe (Number 18 instead of Number 10), Samuel Adams (Number 24 instead of Number 16); Webster (Number 7 instead of Number 16); Jefferson Davis (Number 10 instead of Number 20); and John Jay (Number 9 instead of Number 24). Thus, according to the *Britannica,* values of Washington, John Adams, J. Q Adams, Henry, Samuel Adams, Clay, and Monroe are significantly lower, and the values of Franklin, Hamilton, Jefferson, Webster, Jay, and Jefferson Davis are significantly higher, than in the textbooks.

The cases of Franklin and John Adams are particularly interesting in the light that they throw upon this crude method of equating achievements Franklin as a world figure among Americans, perhaps ranks with Lincoln and Washington, but his specific place in American history is probably more accurately gauged by his position in the textbooks than by his position in the *Britannica*. On the other hand, John Adams influenced American history directly and specifically through the greater part of a long life covering the very significant period just prior to the Revolution, the War of Revolution, the forma-

[1] In this computation the persons having rank in *both* the civil and the military lists were excluded

tive critical period preceding the adoption of the Constitution, and the infancy and youth of the new nation.

In the *Fourteenth Yearbook* of the National Society for the Study of Education (p. 136), the frequencies of reference to certain persons in *periodical literature* are given as illustrative of the results obtained in applying the "newspaper-magazine" method to the determination of minimal essentials in history [1] In so far as the characters of American history are concerned, the frequencies of reference for the first four persons were the same as in the table presented above for those important in the affairs of civil life  Leaving out the three whose prominence is due in whole or in part to events that have transpired since 1865, the list as given in the *Yearbook* is as follows:

| | | | |
|---|---|---|---|
| Lincoln | 100 | Webster | 13 |
| Washington | 66 | Franklin | 10 |
| Jefferson | 51 | J Q Adams | 10 |
| Jackson | 24 | Buchanan | 10 |
| Clay | 20 | | |

In comparing this list with the corresponding list representing frequency of reference in the textbooks, a fair degree of resemblance is to be noted  The first four names are in the same order in both lists, and all of the nine names having the greatest frequencies of reference in the newspapers and magazines are found among the first eighteen in the list based upon frequency of reference in the textbooks.

The total number of names mentioned in the several books varies from 261 in Eggleston to 650 in Woodburn and Moran.  The averages for the different periods show a rather surprising similarity, especially for the two latest periods:

TABLE XXV

| Books of | Average number of names | Range |
|---|---|---|
| Class I | 491 | 410 to 537 |
| Class II | 372 | 261 to 427 |
| Class III | 471 | 365 to 650 |
| Class IV | 471 | 348 to 536 |

In view of the fact that the more recent books are, on the average, one third larger than the earliest books, it is clear that, in proportion to the ground covered, the recent books mention fewer names than the earlier books

[1] The table of frequencies appearing in the *Yearbook* was put forth simply as a suggestion of what the "newspaper magazine" method might accomplish if carried out in greater detail than was possible at the time

## XV

## SUMMARY AND INTERPRETATIONS

The more important facts set forth in the preceding pages may be summarized as follows

1) In so far as can be determined from the materials presented in the textbooks. elementary American history as taught in the seventh and eighth grades has been and still is predominantly political and military history.

2) Within the past fifty years, the emphasis upon military affairs as measured by the proportion of space devoted to wars has declined. In general, battles and campaigns are treated less in detail than was formerly the rule, while proportionately more space is devoted to the causes and the results of wars. The lessening emphasis upon the details of the wars is first noticed in some of the textbooks published between 1881 and 1888, and the tendency has been general and decided since that time

3) The later books give a perceptibly heavier emphasis to the facts of economic and industrial development than do the earlier books, although political development still constitutes the essential core of elementary historical instruction

4) As regards the treatment of specific eras or epochs, the principal increases in emphasis are to be noted in connection with: (a) the period 1783-1812 (especially in the treatment of the so-called "critical period" between the close of the Revolution and the adoption of the Constitution) ; (b) the non-military affairs of the period 1812-1861 ; and (c) European events preceding and during the periods of discovery, exploration, and settlement

5) The persons whose names are most frequently mentioned in the elementary textbooks are very predominantly those who have been most intimately associated with political development and with military and naval affairs.

6) Variations among the several textbooks in respect of persons mentioned are numerous and wide  Most of the books mention a very much larger number of names than the average pupil will be likely to remember. Certain names, however, are made to stand out through repetition  Whether these are the names that should in justice be perpetuated through the powerful agency represented by universal education is a question which it is not the province of this paper to consider

7) Variations in the topics and events which constitute the chief content of elementary historical instruction are probably less numerous

and less wide than variations in names of persons mentioned.  In any
case there is a rather distinct "core" of topics common to most of the
books, and these topics may be looked upon as constituting the present
"standardized" content of elementary American history  Again it is
not the province of this paper to consider the right of these common
topics to the important place that they now occupy as basic elements
in the culture of the next generation.

8)  Numerous changes have taken place in the construction of
elementary textbooks in history during the past fifty years  The more
important of these are. (a) a movement toward a simpler "style"
with larger emphasis upon clear statements of causal relationships;
(b) the introduction and development of the "problem" as a method
of teaching history, and a consequent encouragement of "judgment" as
contrasted with rote memory,—of rational as contrasted with ver-
batim mastery; (c) a marked decline in the employment of imaginative
pictures as illustrations and an increase in the use of pictures that
represent sincere attempts to portray actual conditions, (d) a marked
decline in the use of anecdotal materials; (e) a larger and wider use
of maps.

The present paper will not attempt to discuss the functions that
American history *should* discharge as a part of the curriculum of
elementary education, but it may be permissible to indicate one of the
influences that this subject has been and still is exerting

This indubitable influence is that of *nationalization*.  The elementary textbooks in history as they have been and are now constituted
present a common stock of information concerning the development
of the United States as a nation to an extent that realizes in some
measure the desire of Washington:

> "It has always been my ardent wish to see a plan devised, on a liberal
> scale, which would have the tendency to spread *systematic ideas* through all
> parts of this rising empire, *thereby to do away with local attachments* and
> *State prejudices,* as far as the nature of things would, or indeed ought to,
> admit, *from our national councils* "[1]

With all of their individual characteristics and specific differences
of emphasis, the textbooks in elementary history have probably done
much to discharge this function.  Even the books that have been
written for the schools of the South, while they naturally emphasize
certain events that the northern books either neglect or tend to min-
imize, present the same essential facts regarding the development of

[1]Quoted in Berard's text  The writers have been unable to find this quotation in Ford's
collection of Washington's papers

the nation; and the differences between the book written for the Catholic parochial schools, and the remaining books included in the study, while significant from the point of view of Catholicism, are quite negligible from the nationalistic point of view.

Whether the elementary textbooks tend to engender nationalism or patriotism of an unfortunate type and whether, indeed, any agency that tends to develop nationalistic ideals should be countenanced in education,[1] are questions that this paper cannot discuss. The fact is that the obvious influence of the elementary textbook in history today is distinctly toward the promotion of nationalism through giving to all of the pupils who reach the seventh and eighth years of school life a common stock of information regarding national development. Even though much of this information is forgotten, there can be no doubt that the attitudes and points of view engendered by this systematic study have a profound influence upon collective thought and collective conduct in so far as these are concerned with national problems.

So long as the function of elementary history continues to be predominantly the development of nationalism, the core of historical instruction will probably continue to be the political development of the nation. The movement toward a lessening emphasis of wars, and especially of the details of battles and campaigns, will doubtless go on; the social and industrial changes that have profoundly modified the course of political events will receive larger and larger emphasis; characters other than those concerned with political and military affairs will receive a more adequate recognition, but the essential organization of events around the unifying thread of political development is probably inevitable. If the primary function of history is otherwise conceived, however, and if the new conception is acceptable to the people, another type of organization may be, and doubtless will be, devised, other kinds of facts will form the content of instruction; and other names will replace those that now occupy the favored niches in the "Hall of Fame."

The important question at the present juncture would seem to center about the desirability or undesirability of making the development of nationalism the primary function of seventh and eighth grade history. This is an issue that is fraught with consequences far too fundamental to be settled by any single group of individuals. Historians and educationists, as single groups or cooperatively, may raise the question, but the decision must rest with the people. In view of the present tendency to reorganize the seventh and eighth grades, and

---

[1] An explicit discouragement of nationalism was recommended by the National Education Association in the resolutions adopted at the Oakland meeting in August, 1915

(under the junior-high-school proposals) to provide differentiated curriculums beginning with the seventh grade, the question of the function of elementary history assumes large importance  Curriculums in which history does not appear at all have been proposed, as well as curriculums which provide different varieties of history to meet so-called "interests" (industrial history replacing political history for those "destined" for industrial occupations, for example)  The bearing of policies such as these upon national life should at least be recognized.

If the function of elementary history remains substantially what it has been in the past and what it is to-day, there will still be room for large improvement in the content and in the methods of instruction, but it is highly probable that some of the needs brought out by recent criticisms of historical instruction will have to be met in other ways  If the primacy of nationalism is admitted, there is little hope for fulfilling this function and still effecting marked curtailments of the present content  If essentially larger emphases upon local history, upon recent history, and upon the development of art, literature, science, and industry are demanded, it would seem that they must be provided for outside of the time and space now devoted to history in the seventh and eighth grades, for to compress into the present time and space the details essential both to fulfill the present function and to meet these additional needs would certainly tend to defeat every purpose which the teaching of the subject might otherwise accomplish.